Dreams That Die

Misadventures In Hollywood

Dreams That Die

Misadventures In Hollywood

John Wight

Winchester, UK
Washington, USA

First published by Zero Books, 2013
Zero Books is an imprint of John Hunt Publishing Ltd., Laurel House, Station Approach,
Alresford, Hants, SO24 9JH, UK
office1@jhpbooks.net
www.johnhuntpublishing.com
www.zero-books.net

For distributor details and how to order please visit the 'Ordering' section on our website.

ISBN: 978 1 84694 712 4

A CIP catalogue record for this book is available from the British Library.

Design: Stuart Davies

Printed and bound by CPI Group (UK) Ltd, Croydon, CR0 4YY

CONTENTS

Hollywood is a place where they'll pay you a thousand dollars for a kiss and fifty cents for your soul.

Marilyn Monroe

1

If I had any notion of what being an extra in Hollywood involved, it began to dissipate as soon as I arrived at the offices of Central Casting in Burbank one oppressively hot morning to register as one, and was introduced to the reality.

The place was jam-packed with people who like me had come to register as extras (officially referred to within the industry as 'background artists'). They occupied every available inch of space - some sitting at long tables filling out registration forms picked up from the tray on the way in; others chatting excitedly in various groups; still more standing in a long queue that ran the entire length of the room, made up of those who'd already completed their forms and were now waiting to have them processed. We consisted of all types in terms of age, gender, ethnicity, and physical appearance. The younger guys were all trying to appear cool, while the girls were dressed to look their best. Meanwhile the more mature stood or sat quietly, as if contemplating a future that was no longer theirs to control.

On the registration form, apart from the obligatory personal details - address, phone number, email, age, measurements etc. you were asked about any special talents you might have; about any costumes or uniforms owned; the style and make of your automobile; whether you'd be willing to appear on camera semi-naked or nude; and about whether you would have any problems working on set with smoke, animals, and so forth.

Quickly filling mine out with fabrication after fabrication (yes, I can ride a horse; yes, I have had firearms training), I took my place at the back of the queue of people waiting to hand over their twenty-five dollar registration fee, have their picture taken, and be added to the agency's vast database.

Half an hour later, duly signed up and processed, I emerged from the office a non-union extra. In my hand I had a list of numbers to call when checking in for work, the names and addresses of studio lots located all the way from Burbank to Santa Monica, along with a list of do's and don'ts.

Do be on time. *Do* take something to read. *Do* pay attention and listen to instructions while on set. *Do* take wardrobe choices (always pressed and neat in a garment bag and never rolled up in a duffel bag). *Do* arrive on set hair and makeup ready unless otherwise instructed.

As for the don'ts: *Do not* cancel a booking without good reason and without leaving the casting director enough time to replace you. *Do not* under any circumstances approach any of the principal actors for an autograph or for any other reason on set.

Do not attempt to bring a camera or recording equipment of any kind with you to the set. *Do not* leave the set without informing someone. *Do not* talk on set unless otherwise instructed. *Do not* look directly into the camera unless otherwise instructed.

Now that you've signed up, paid your money and had your picture taken, it's time to book a job. You did this by calling the special work-line phone number you'd just been given, making sure it was the one that corresponded to your category - which in my case was non-union men - and trying to grab something.

What you got when calling was a long recorded message made up of a series of personal messages from the many different casting directors at Central, looking for people to work the particular show for which they were responsible for booking extras.

For example:

'Hey guys, this is Chad. I need military-types, late twenties/early thirties, in good shape for a SWAT team. Firearms experience is an advantage but not necessary. It's for NYPD Blue and it works tomorrow and possibly Thursday. If you fit this category call me on ...'

'Hi fellas, Tony here. Today I'm looking for young, hip New

York types for the new episode of Law and Order. It works two days, possibly three. If that's you give me a call on ...'

When you called looking for work, if you were lucky you might get straight through to the casting director concerned. Usually you were greeted with the busy tone and would have to try countless times before you were successful. When you got through you were immediately asked for your social security number (the US equivalent to a national insurance number). Punching this into a computer brought up your file and picture. If the casting director thought you looked and/or were what they were looking for, they'd book you. They might then – but not always - give you a call time (the time you're required to be on set for work), along with another number to call for wardrobe details, location and travel directions, in addition to any other relevant information. At this point you were also given an extension number to access the 'call-time change box.' This you called before going to bed the night before the day of the job and again first thing in the morning in case the call time had changed. If it had changed you received the new call time in a recorded message.

After you'd gone through all of the above - had managed to get through on the work line and found yourself a show, then got through to the relevant casting director and got booked, then called the information line to get your call time, wardrobe instructions and location, then checked the call-time change box to find out if there'd been any change to your original call time - then and only then were you ready to work.

My first ever booking was on an Aaron Spelling soap. I don't remember the name of the show now, which I believe was cancelled after only two or three episodes, but I do recall the scene I was in. It was shot on location somewhere in Pasadena and it was a night shoot. I got there ten or fifteen minutes late, having taken the wrong freeway exit, and as timekeeping is drummed into you by the casting directors like the catechism is drummed into a Catholic, I arrived dripping with sweat and out of breath, half expecting to be summarily put to death.

Luckily, the production assistant whose job it was to organize and sign in the extras when they arrived hardly took notice of the time. Instead she just handed me my voucher and without so much as a glance in my direction pointed the way to the wardrobe trailer and the line of people already waiting there.

Voucher in hand (a voucher is your timesheet. At the end of each day it is signed by both yourself and the production assistant to verify that you worked the hours stated. You are given a copy for your records, the production company keeps a copy for theirs, with the third copy sent by the production company to the payroll company, from where your cheque is sent out a week or so later). I did as directed and trooped off much relieved.

Along with my fellow extras, I waited my turn to be checked over by the wardrobe department. I was conscious of this being my first-ever time on a set and these people my first exposure to working extras. I have to say we were a strange-looking bunch, mostly down-at-heel desperate-looking characters dressed in ill-fitting clothes. The wardrobe lady - almost always in a foul mood I was to learn through long experience - was checking the clothes that each extra had brought with them, instructing them what to wear. If she didn't like the choices brought, she went into the trailer and brought out alternatives from the production's own stock.

Picking through each extra's clothes, she had an expression of unalloyed contempt on her face, as if she were picking through radioactive waste. By the time it came my turn I'd built myself up to be abused as the poor woman in front of me just had:

'Is this all you have? Weren't you told to bring two changes? Look at these pants. They're full of creases. Jesus Christ!'

I was lucky. She passed me without asking to see any of the choices I'd brought. Yes, I remember thinking. The gods are with me.

Once you'd checked in, been through the trauma of wardrobe inspection and changed (if instructed to do so), you were then directed to extras-holding, the specially designated area on every production where the extras sit around and wait until they are called to the set to work in a scene. Here people typically read, listen to music, play cards and/or engage in hushed conversations. Many extras, obviously old hands at the game, bring their own fold-up chairs, while others don't bother and instead endure the uncomfortable plastic ones provided by the production company. Production companies were only obliged to provide chairs for union extras, not non-union, which for those like me who were non-union only served to emphasise our lowly status by comparison.

Thankfully, on this my first experience of extra work the production company made no distinction between both categories of extras, as most didn't when it came to this particular rule, and I found myself sat in extras-holding beside a guy who was originally from Jordan on one side and an older lady who was Orange County-white on the other. With the lady engrossed in knitting to pass the time, I struck up a conversation with Ahmed, who was soon telling me his story.

He had left Jordan in search of a better future when he was in his early twenties. He spent a few years in Europe before heading Stateside, his home now for the past two decades. Stamped on his face was all the evidence of a man acquainted with life's ups and downs. He drove a cab in New York for five years and was robbed countless times. His luck changed when his father, whom he hadn't seen or spoken to in years, died leaving him a chunk of money. It was enough to set up a sandwich shop.

Business was good at first - so good that after a couple of years he acquired a business partner and together they opened another five shops, dotted around Manhattan. However, things began to go wrong when Ahmed caught his partner stealing from the business. Though he succeeded in forcing him out, his former partner was determined not to go quietly. He planted vermin in a couple of the shops before making an anonymous phone call to the health inspector. They arrived unannounced one day and promptly shut Ahmed down. The ensuing publicity killed off any hopes of the business continuing, prompting him to move out to LA to make a fresh start.

I soon became disconcerted as Ahmed bemoaned life as an extra. He'd been working full-time non-union for just over a year by now, having gambled away the last of his savings in Vegas, and he had no hesitation in informing me that he hated every second. When I attempted to cheer him up by pointing out there was always the chance of things changing for the better, of the opportunities for success that exist in Hollywood, he offered a derisory laugh in response.

'Forget about such illusions, my friend. It will never happen. Never. Anyone who thinks otherwise is either insane or doesn't know what they're talking about.'

Thankfully, before the conversation could continue, the production assistant arrived to take us to the set.

Within a production crew there are only a few people entrusted with the thankless task of placing and directing the extras in a scene. In order of importance they are the second assistant director (also know as the key-second), the second-second assistant director (second-second), and the production assistant (PA). The scene we were in was set outside a theater, with the extras playing theater-goers emerging at the end of a performance. The second-second quickly went round pairing us up into couples. To my disappointment I found myself paired with a woman who looked old enough to be my mother.

The principal actors were a couple of Ken and Barbie looka-likes, no doubt destined for rehab, and they strutted around the set with not a hair out of place, glow-in-the-dark teeth, and an entourage of makeup and hair ladies fawning all over them.

My pretend-partner and I were placed so far away from the action we needed the production assistant to relay the directions to us specifically from a position off to the side behind a pillar. The woman I'd been paired with seemed very shy and withdrawn, but as we had been directed to walk arm-in-arm I decided to pursue a conversation regardless, if only to break the ice. Her reaction to my accent was one I would get used to in Hollywood - a combination of deep surprise and curiosity, as if the person concerned had just happened upon a near-distinct species in the wild.

'Wow, you're from Scaht-land?'

'Yes.'

'Wow.'

'Indeed.'

'How long you been out here?' I told her.

'How do you like it so far?'

'It's good. Not bad. You know…different.'

'You come here for acting?'

'Well ...'

'You in the union yet?'

'No, not yet. You?'

'No. My tits aren't big enough. That's who gets the vouchers. Young chicks with big tits.'

'I see.'

2

By the time I started working as an extra I had been in LA just over three months, arriving in the summer of 2000 from Scotland with the aim of establishing a career as a screenwriter. Being a screenwriter in Scotland, I'd come to realize, was like being a cactus in the North Pole. In my early thirties, with no career and precious little in the way of savings or assets, it was time to either give it up for an occupation that was more attainable at home, or take my chances and head out to Hollywood to see if I could make it happen.

After a concerted period of deliberation and uncertainty, I decided to use up the last of my savings and take the plunge. My reasoning came down to this: I was single, had no commitments or responsibilities other than myself, and I would always regret not giving it a go if I decided to give up. Then there was the fact I'd already been to LA, spending a year there five or six years previously, and therefore more or less knew what I was letting myself in for. That said, this was as much a negative as a positive factor when it came to making my decision to return.

My previous time there had ended in me returning home flat broke after losing my job and breaking up with the girl I'd been living with. Back then I'd already had a latent desire to work in the movie industry. But nothing in my experience or upbringing had endowed me with the belief that I could. The social conditioning I'd been through in this regard had impacted me in ways I wasn't even conscious of at the time. I even recall being reluctant to even share these thoughts with any of my friends or family for fear of being ridiculed. During my previous spell in LA I'd worked hard to suppress the urge to take a different path in life, instead accepting a fate of working in any job I could get my hands on and learning to make do. I had no formal education to speak of, had never gone to university, nor had I ever served an apprenticeship in a trade. In other words, my career choices were limited.

It was meeting David, a Welsh guy around my age during that initial stint in LA, which inspired me to finally to start doing what I wanted in life rather than continue to remain dissatisfied and frustrated in the meaningless, unfulfilling occupations I'd worked at since leaving school. I ran into him at the King George in Santa Monica, where I used to go for a drink after work two or three times a week.

At the time I was managing a sports store in the Santa Monica Place shopping mall, located at one end of the Third Street Promenade, a bustling shopping precinct popular with tourists. I was being shafted by the owner, a fellow Scot by the name of Howard Shaw, who' d sold his chain of sports stores back home and decamped to Palm Springs to enjoy an early retirement. He decided after a year of sitting by the pool to open a new sports store in Santa Monica - just to keep his hand in. Mind you, he still spent his days sitting by the pool. The only difference now was that he interrupted his day with three phone calls to the store - one in the morning, one at lunch time, and one in the evening - to find out how much money he was making. When the figures weren't as good as he felt they should be, he'd want to know why.

Perhaps I could have put up with his shite if he was paying me a decent salary. He wasn't. On the contrary, he was paying me a pittance. In time, reluctant to keep the place properly stocked, the store would go to the wall. Before it did Howard planned to do a moonlight, turning up with a truck to clear the place late one night before disappearing. The rent was behind, none of the suppliers were being paid, and he informed me on the q.t. that he wanted it kept quiet from the rest of the staff, who hadn't been paid in weeks by this point either and whom he intended to leave high and dry. Most of them were college kids who were working at the store part time to help pay their way through school. Howard told me he was going to give me a bonus for helping him carry out his plan.

This was his mistake.

I gathered the staff together and told them what was happening, what the owner's intentions were, and made sure they were paid in kind - i.e. by helping themselves to the stock.

By the time Howard turned up with a truck and two Mexican workers to clear the place out a couple of weeks later, there was hardly enough left to fill the cab up front never mind the back.

But I digress.

The King George was located a short walk from the mall along the Third Street Promenade. It was popular with many of the ex-pats who called Santa Monica home. In time I would view it as a sad scene, but that time still lay some way off. At the time I still enjoyed going there to sample a taste of the culture I'd left behind.

Originally from Cardiff, David was the head doorman there. Like me he'd been brought up on a housing estate and wanted something better out of life. Unlike me he was in the process of making a movie. That's right, here was someone from a similar background to my own, with no formal education or training in making films, declaring his intention of doing exactly that.

On my days off I would visit him at the office he worked out of on Wilshire Boulevard, where he'd set up his own production company. David was popular within the ex-pat community, as were the regular parties he threw at his house close to Venice Beach. They typically lasted long into the night, with people packed in his front garden drinking beer and dancing while breathing in the ocean air under a clear night sky. It was a long way from Scotland.

Despite living in the movie capital of the world, it was only when I returned home as a result of circumstances beyond my control that I set out to master the craft of screenwriting. Embracing the clarity of knowing at last what I wanted to do with my life, I rented a cheap flat in Edinburgh, signed on the dole, and embarked on a daily routine of writing and reading. My output was prodigious, even though I had no idea if what I was producing was good enough to be taken seriously. When not at my desk writing on the old, second-hand word processor I'd managed to obtain, I spent hours in bookshops poring through the myriad books on screenwriting contained in the Film & TV section. I also read the published screenplays of classic movies, hoping to imbibe whatever it was that made them classics.

Doggedly sticking to this routine, in four years I managed to complete five feature-length screenplays along with numerous scripts for short films. But if I thought after this that my task was complete, I was wrong. Now I was faced with the monumental task of getting them read by agents and producers. Surviving on the tight budget of a fortnightly dole cheque and savings that were slowly but surely ebbing away, I could only afford incoming calls on my landline (this was in the days before mobile phones became the norm). This meant that any outgoing phone calls I wanted or needed to make had to be made from the public phone box located at the end of the street. Day after day there I'd be, calling the offices of literary agents and producers in London, trying to persuade them to look at my work, fighting a losing battle with the noise of the traffic and on more than on occasion pneumatic drills and other construction equipment in the background. It was a Promethean struggle but one that I never, even for a second, considered giving up on. This I'd decided was to be my path in life, and I was determined to walk it to the end.

In those first years I must have received over a hundred letters of rejection, comprising a short paragraph informing me that while the agent or production company in question thanked me for the opportunity of reading my work, they were afraid they did not feel strongly enough about the material to take matters further. I saved them in a file, looking forward to the day when I could call them up to rub their noses in it after winning some prestigious award or other. But as time passed and all I had to show for my monastic work schedule was this ever-bulging file of rejection letters, I realized I was deluding myself if I thought I could crack the movie industry from Edinburgh. This sense of futility was added to by my experience of the annual Edinburgh International Film Festival.

I attended it three years running, and on each occasion felt completely out of place. The people there, with their Oxbridge accents and trendy clothes, with their satchels and their confident swaggers, weren't like me. In fact, I felt so out of place I came away from the experience each time questioning what I was doing and whether or not I should just give in to a fate of working in a job I hated for the rest of my life.

But each time I experienced such doubts, following close behind would come renewed determination in the shape of anger at a world that appeared determined to keep me in some predetermined box. No way was I going to give up. No matter how tough it was or how long it took, I was going to make my living as a screenwriter.

By my fourth year of zero success I was forced to make a hard choice. My work may have improved to the point where agents and producers were now replying with more than a single paragraph form-letter rejecting it out of hand, but a breakthrough towards anything resembling a career remained elusive. One event in particular illustrates how frustrating the process had become.

A certain producer who'd read my work liked it enough to pass on to one of the more prestigious literary agencies in the business, based in London. The agent within the agency who read the script also liked it and requested another sample to help them make up their mind whether to take me on or not. I sent it off to them convinced I could now sit back and look forward to the success I fully deserved after putting in four long years of dedication to the craft.

I was wrong.

Indeed, not only was I wrong I was handed a harsh lesson on the nature of an industry in which the word 'deserve' doesn't exist. It wasn't that the agent read the second script and informed me that they had decided not to take me on after all. It was that she read it and didn't even deign to reply. I had already established telephone contact with her after she read the initial script and raved about it. Now when I tried calling to find out what she thought about the second script my calls went straight to voicemail. On each occasion I left a polite message requesting an update on any news concerning the script. Bear in mind that this was a couple of months after I'd sent it in, leaving her more than enough time to give it the once-over. I then tried writing to her, again asking what the status was, assuring her that I understood if she'd decided to pass but to let me know either way in order to bring closure to the matter. The letter went unanswered.

Pissed off, I got back on the phone. This time when the receptionist tried putting me through to the agent's voicemail I refused and instead told her to pass on the message that I was on my way down to London to collect my scripts in person and that they had better be ready for collection when I arrived. I then put the phone down, grabbed my coat, threw a couple of things into a bag, went straight to the station and purchased a ticket on the next train to London.

Most of the five hour-journey I spent visualizing arriving at the agency's office, barging through the door and bringing the place to a standstill with the verbal assault of righteous indignation I was intent on unleashing. The train pulled into Kings Cross Station and I joined a massive wave of alienated humanity heading for the station concourse. I made my way down the stairs into the underground and jumped on the Tube. I re-emerged at Covent Garden straight into a downpour. By the time I'd located the building in which the agency had its office I was soaked to the bone. They were on the fourth floor, but I never made it past the security guard in the foyer. He asked my name, I told him, whereupon he handed me a brown padded envelope containing my scripts before bidding me a polite but firm farewell.

It was while returning to Scotland on the train an hour or so later that I decided it was time to either give up or take drastic action in the form of moving to Hollywood for a last-ditch effort at making the goal of a career writing films a reality. All I had to show for four years of dedication and persistence was that bulging file of rejection letters I've already mentioned and a short film I'd written and co-produced. The real drama during the aforementioned project had taken place behind rather than in front of the camera, with a series of arguments, fall outs, and tantrums all the way through. Worse, the female lead actor committed suicide not long after we finished shooting, though nobody was suggesting both were in any way connected. But it illustrated the atmosphere of doom that surrounded the project from beginning to end. Even having the film screened at the London Film Festival failed to compensate for the trauma involved in making the fucking thing.

So, yes, by the time the train pulled into Edinburgh my mind was made up.

Hollywood here I come.

3

From the moment I made my mind up it took three months to get everything organized.

On my previous sojourn to LA I had rented an apartment on Sycamore Avenue, just off Hollywood Boulevard, a street which back then consisted of a transient population of students, wannabe actors, writers and others who'd just arrived and needed cheap accommodation. There was also a liberal sprinkling of those who lived here simply because they were down on their luck and unable to afford anything better.

All along Sycamore the apartment buildings gleamed under the sun, while the street was lined on either side by palm trees. It was a façade which belied an underbelly of poverty and broken humanity. Nighttime brought out the crack dealers, who occupied various street corners. They were part of the local Mexican street gang who ruled the area as a king rules his kingdom, and were not to be messed with. Fortunately they weren't interested in bothering anyone who didn't bother them, and after a few weeks my face became known and I'd be greeted with a perfunctory nod as I passed them on my way to and from the apartment.

But where there are crack dealers there are crack heads, and anytime I came across one of them I would up the pace and keep my head down in the knowledge that where they were concerned anything can happen.

At the bottom of the street, on the corner of Hollywood Boulevard, a grand opulent building spoke of money, power and influence. It was one of many such buildings dotted in and around Hollywood, all of them owned and occupied by the Church of Scientology. Most nights a police chopper hovered overhead, shining its spotlight on the streets below in its search for crimes and fugitives from the law, while during the day

Hollywood Boulevard itself was always chock-a-block with a strange combination of street performers, tourists, and assorted street people waiting for an opportunity to part them from their money.

However the main thing is that accommodation here was both cheap and familiar, which is why as soon as I made it through immigration and emerged from LAX into the warmth of a typical LA afternoon, I jumped on a shuttle bus and headed straight there. I had enough money with me to put down a deposit and pay the first month's rent on something cheap. Beyond that I was toast.

A week after my arrival I was ensconced in a studio apartment that was so small you'd be forgiven for expecting the toilet to flush whenever someone pressed the doorbell. It comprised one main room, off of which lay a tiny kitchen area, shower cubicle and toilet. Fortunately it was clean, freshly painted, and contained everything required for a bare existence apart from air conditioning, a must-have amenity during the sweltering months of an LA summer.

Furniture consisted of bits and pieces I purchased for seventy bucks from the manager of the building, all second-hand items left behind by previous tenants. It included a mattress to sleep on, which I stuck in one corner on the floor, a small writing desk, and a small telephone table. This, along with sundry other items I purchased from the discount store down the street - bed linen, kitchen utensils, plates and cups, a telephone, and so on - constituted the extent of my belongings. I had no television or music system, which meant that my one source of entertainment was the small selection of books I'd packed. I had two boxes of books and a box containing more clothes being shipped over, but they wouldn't arrive for another few weeks.

My neighbours were an odd bunch. On my right lived a young Hispanic guy by the name of Nick. I'd only just moved in when he made a point of knocking on the door and introducing himself. He was an actor and stand-up comedian and you always heard him before you saw him. He had a girlfriend who often stayed over. The two of them liked to have it away at all hours of the night and the noise would keep me awake, the paper-thin walls ensuring that I heard every grunt and groan.

Opposite Nick lived an old guy named Pete. He was a Vietnam vet who always had a friendly greeting and liked to stop for a quick chat every time he passed. During these short exchanges he never failed to introduce the topic of politics, complaining about 'those damned liberals and commies in the White House.' I was never able to understand how anyone could describe George W Bush as a liberal or a communist. But then again who was I to argue with a man who'd been wounded in combat and who went out of his way to mention that he kept a fully loaded .44 Magnum in his apartment, 'just in case.'

The rest of the landing was made up of an aspiring rock guitarist, a struggling novelist named Richard who walked fourteen miles a day every day in-between writing, and a girl called Destiny who worked as a lapdancer at a strip club down the street. We were an eclectic bunch, a microcosm of Hollywood and the strange personalities the place attracts from all over the world. The important thing is that we all got along.

After spending a week or so getting settled in, I turned my attention to finding a job. The money I had with me was only enough to keep me going for a couple of months and I was conscious of the danger of sitting back and waiting until it ran out before doing something about it. The stability that a regular income would provide was important, as was getting out and meeting people, which is why one bright morning I put on a smart shirt and my one pair of smart trousers before heading for the Mondrian Hotel, slap bang in the middle of the Sunset Strip. A boutique hotel popular with members of Hollywood's glitterati - actors, producers, directors, agents etc, along with the ubiquitous hangers-on desperate to gain their attention - where better for an aspiring screenwriter to meet people in positions of influence?

And given that it was near impossible to gain entry to the Skybar, the bar located inside the hotel where those assorted Hollywood VIPs congregated most nights, surely the next best thing would be to gain employment there and get paid for the privilege.

One of the positive aspects to moving halfway across the world to a place where you don't know anyone and no one knows you, is that it frees you from worrying about what other people think. I would never have considered, even for a second, walking into a hotel back home to ask for a job as a doorman. In fact, I wouldn't have allowed myself to work as a doorman at all. The opprobrium that would come my way from people who knew me would have been too much to bear. Back home I had worked as a doorman/bouncer in bars and clubs in my late teens and early twenties, and had had more than had my fill of it by the time I quit. Going back to this line of work in my home town in my early thirties would have been tantamount to a public declaration of regression.

There was no such dilemma to wrestle with in LA, however. On the contrary, walking into the Mondrian past the bellhops and valets outside in their cream linen suits, and passing through the hotel's swanky foyer on my way over to reception, the adrenalin was flowing. As soon as I walked in I knew that this was the place to be. It reeked of opportunity and opportunity is what I was about.

Extending this wisdom further, they say that in life you make your own luck, and they also say that fortune favours the brave. And while both may be well worn clichés, in my first few weeks in the movie capital of the world they proved correct. I'd arrived at the Mondrian Hotel on the Sunset Strip looking for work as a doorman without having been apprised of there being any vacancies beforehand. I hadn't called in advance and I had not been invited to come in for an interview. I did not know a soul who worked in the place, and yet within half an hour of arriving at reception and making tentative inquiries, there I was, seated in the security office with Albert the head of security being interviewed for a vacant position for a job. Turns out I had arrived at the right time. Hotel security were a couple of bodies short after one guy quit and another was fired - though for what I never found out.

Albert was an avuncular figure, a former college football linebacker gone to seed. He liked to talk a lot and I warmed to him easily. In fact, from that first meeting I knew the job was mine. The truth is, however, it would have been anybody's who was tall and appeared fairly fit and presentable.

The security office was located in the underground parking garage. I was introduced there to a couple of the guys who worked the day shift, after which Albert took me on a quick tour of the hotel and the Skybar. Along the way he talked about his relationship with a Filipino woman he'd met working at his other job (Albert, it turned out, was head of security at both the Mondrian and a Marriott Hotel on Wilshire Boulevard. He worked both jobs full time, alternating shift patterns, which probably explained why he shuffled everywhere instead of walked and always appeared ready to collapse from a lack of sleep).

By day the Skybar doubled as a poolside bar with a spectacular view out over LA via a massive picture window that ran the entire length of one wall. Hotel guests were dotted around the pool on sun loungers partaking of the refreshments brought them by a small army of cocktail waiters and waitresses. The waitresses were attired in figure-hugging Hawaiian-type dresses and each seemed more beautiful than the last. All of them were budding models and actresses who'd relocated to LA from all over the US and beyond, chasing the dream.

There was an enclosed lounge area in the far corner, which

you reached by climbing a set of wooden stairs. As he led me up for a look, Albert explained how at night the place is so packed you can hardly move. He also took pains to point out that to work here you had to have a calm temperament. Due to the popularity of the place, you invariably rejected more people at the entrance to the bar than you let in, and as a result you could expect to be on the receiving end of lots of verbal abuse from the kind of people who don't take kindly to being told no. Of course, I took pains to assure Albert that here standing before him was the very epitome of calm, citing and exaggerating my long experience working security at all manner of events back in the UK, including big open-air rock concerts, bars, nightclubs, and even VIP security. He seemed impressed and by the end of the brief tour told me he was going to recommend me to the hotel's general manager, who would call in a day or so to arrange a formal interview.

Fast forward a week later and there I am, standing at the entrance to the Skybar suited and booted on my first night on the job. I've got a radio in my hand as I watch Dave, the doorman-cum-host, checking people off the guest list he has laid out on the plinth in front of him. The Skybar employed its own security independent of the hotel, and our role as hotel security was to back them up during the hours when the Skybar was busiest, generally from around nine at night through to two in the morning, when the bar closed.

Like the rest of the guys who worked security for the Skybar, Dave was the very essence of cool. Dressed in black from head to toe, standing a lean six-four with a thick mop of blond hair styled in the fashion of the day, he was a dead ringer for a young Clint Eastwood. From Chicago, he'd moved to LA to be an actor and he possessed the charisma and self-confidence of a guy who felt he had the world by the balls.

There was also Matt from New York. He only worked at the Skybar part time, though not to augment the money he made the rest of the week as a male model but rather as an opportunity to be around the multitude of beautiful women who filled the place every weekend.

Big Stu was Australian, stood six feet seven inches tall and had the physique to match. His role was to roam around inside the bar mingling with the customers and generally keeping an eye on things. He and I soon struck up a friendship and would often get together when we weren't working for coffee and such like. He always had a smile on his face and a hundred business cards in his pocket. Determined to get somewhere in life, he viewed his job at the Skybar as an opportunity to network as a business consultant. Despite the many failed projects he got involved in he never lost his optimism and hunger to succeed. In the Skybar his size and gregarious personality made him popular with the regulars.

Among my colleagues working hotel security were Tim and Sean, another two budding actors. Tim was from Philadelphia. He had the worst sense of humour I've ever come across and liked to recount stories of sexual exploits that in the telling you could tell had attained the level of fantasy. As for Sean, he'd moved to LA from Seattle via a stint in the Marines. He was convinced it was his destiny to be the next Denzel Washington. I'll say this for him, he came close. The director credited with discovering Denzel, Spike Lee, came into the Skybar one night and Sean got talking to him. Lee liked him enough to give him an audition for a small part in the pilot of a new TV show he was producing. Alas, the pilot didn't get picked up and Sean was returned to the obscurity from whence he came.

In addition to those there were others I've since forgotten, mostly guys who worked the day shift or part time at the weekend.

I worked at the Mondrian full time five nights a week. Three of those nights my shift began at four and lasted through to midnight. The other two nights, Friday and Saturday, I started at eleven and worked through to seven the next morning, when the dayshift kicked in. The craziest period came during the nightshift in the hour immediately after the Skybar closed, when we set about the task of clearing everyone out of the hotel. On Friday and Saturday nights it was mayhem, with people, mostly drunk and/or high on something, trying to get up to the hotel rooms for impromptu parties. The elevators in the foyer became a virtual battlefield as we stood guard in front of them, inspecting room keys to try and ensure that only hotel guests passed into the elevators and on up to the rooms. We were always outnumbered and found ourselves being harassed, abused and jostled by an angry and determined crowd, the kind of people whose respect for hotel doormen and security guards was less than zero and who as a result refused to take no for an answer.

By the time the madness ended we were always done in, mentally and physically drained after having endured two hours of arguing, pushing, and the verbal abuse and angry imprecations of a baying mob. I'd go and find a seat and rest for fifteen minutes or so, before the first calls began to come through on the radio for security to respond to complaints of noise emanating from various rooms throughout the hotel. Inevitably, despite our efforts, some people always managed to succeed in getting past and on up to the rooms to carry on where they'd left off in the Skybar.

Led by Albert, there were usually around four of us making up the team tasked with breaking up these impromptu parties and ejecting non-hotel guests. It sometimes necessitated the use of force, with people apt to become angry and frustrated at having their night ruined. Albert took the lead in these situations. The rest of us would line up alongside him as the hotel room door in question opened and the drama began. This part of the night could last anywhere from just fifteen minutes to over an hour, depending on how many after-parties we had to deal with. Once it ended whoever was scheduled to work through to the next morning was on their lonesome until seven a.m.

Patrolling a hotel through the long, lonely hours of the night is a surreal experience. Two foot patrols of the Mondrian were mandatory on nightshift duty, which given the size of the place meant spending most of the shift walking around inspecting every nook and cranny of the place.

Beginning in the parking garage in the basement, you gradually worked your way up through each of the hotel's six floors. Your only recourse in the event of anything happening was radio contact with the night manager, whom, I soon learned, spent a large part of the night sleeping in his office. It was a lonely yet at the same time peaceful experience, affording you the opportunity to think.

This was especially the case upon reaching the roof.

Stepping through the emergency exit door to the roof transported you into a different world. Up there it was pitch black and the sound of the traffic below was reduced to a distant hum. You had a torch to help guide the way, but the darkness was so thick the light from it only succeeded in making a dent.

But then, after a few minutes, senses adjusting to the darkness and the height, you began to relax. It was now that you looked out at an ocean of twinkling lights and neon stretched out before you, which in its enormity immediately set the blood pumping through your veins, leaving you awestruck.

With the sun's arrival in the morning I always felt as if I was emerging from a tomb. I'd typically take in the sunrise from the main entrance alongside the valets and the busboys, soaking up the warmth as guests started to appear and like a massive turbine the machinery of the hotel slowly kicked into operation.

When my replacement arrived at seven, I'd punch out, walk to the bus stop along the street and hop on the bus for the short journey along Sunset to La Brea. Sometimes I'd stop off at the mini mall on the corner and grab a coffee and something to eat while leafing through a newspaper before heading home. Mostly

I was too tired to do anything except head straight for the apartment. By the time I'd undressed and showered to wash the night out of me, the mattress on the floor never looked or felt so good.

4

When the Dutch football international Edgar Davids turned up at the Mondrian Hotel I was star struck. It was the summer of 2000 and he was in LA to relax and unwind with his girlfriend after Holland were knocked out in the semis of that year's European Championhsips. Never mind the De Niros and the Pacinos, here was a legend of the beautiful game. My fellow hotel security guards didn't have a clue who he was, which wasn't a surprise given the lack of interest in soccer as a mass spectator sport in the US at that time. To my mind this only made it all the more imperative that I show him the utmost respect and due deference which his status as a footballing genius deserved.

Things started well enough. Davids would come into the Skybar for a few drinks with his girlfriend and a couple of friends, whereupon I would greet him at the entrance and escort him and his party to a table; not just any old table, mind you, but the best in the house, from which you were afforded a panoramic view of LA and its endless tapestry of light and magic.

But then, a week or so into his stay, his girlfriend started acting up. Like the non-famous partners and spouses of many celebrities, she had it fixed in her mind that she too merited VIP treatment on her own terms. We'd already crossed swords when she attempted to use a digital camera to film random people in the hotel. This was a strict no-no given the bar's popularity with celebrities, and after the manager came running over to me panicking I followed him out to the hotel foyer, where she was in the process of recording a group of people in reception as they were checking in. She was drunk and became abusive when I asked her to stop. The manager and staff were watching me.

What to do? Her famous boyfriend was nowhere to be seen.

Finally, fortunately, one of her friends arrived to inform her that their cab had arrived to take them to some party or nightclub somewhere. A couple of nights later she approached the entrance to the Skybar, again having had too much to drink. All of a sudden she was in my face, berating me for having had the gall to tell her to stop filming two nights ago. And who the fuck did I think I was, she screamed, pointing in my face. Do you know who my boyfriend is? You're nothing but a loser doorman. On she went in the same vein. I tried to calm her down, as did Tim beside me, but she kept on. It had been a particularly stressful shift, during which the verbal abuse we'd endured had been worse than usual. Finally I lost my cool and told her to beat it inside or I wouldn't let her in.

Immediately after she stormed off a tall, attractive woman appeared in front of me, pressing her tits up against my chest. The resulting exchange proceeded as follows:

Her: 'Excuse me, I have the New Jersey Nets and their wives with me tonight. This shouldn't present a problem, should it?'

Me: 'Are you or your party guests of the hotel, madam?'

Her: 'No, but we are on the guest list and those are the New Jersey Nets? You have heard of the New Jersey Nets NBA basketball team, haven't you?'

Me: 'I'm afraid you've come to the wrong entrance. The entrance for guest-list customers is outside on Sunset Boulevard. This entrance is for hotel guests only.'

Her: 'We were at the other entrance, but there's a line. I don't think it's appropriate to keep these particular guests waiting, do you?'

Me: 'This entrance is for hotel guests only. I'm afraid you're going to have to go back round to the other entrance.'

Her: 'You mean to tell me that you - a doorman - are going to refuse the New Jersey Nets entry? I'm the West Coast PR Officer for Louis Vuitton. Here's my card. You have heard of Louis Vuitton, haven't you?'

Me: 'I couldn't give a shit if you work for Louis Armstrong, madam. You're not coming in this entrance.'

She hit me with some choice insults and left with her party in tow. She was replaced moments later by one angry Dutch international soccer star and another guy, intent on taking me to task over my sharp exchange with his girlfriend minutes before.

'Hey, chulo, whassup?!' Davids said, squaring up to me.

'Right ya wee cunt…ootside.'

I unclipped the radio from my belt and handed it to Tim beside me. I then made my way through the hotel foyer, through the main door and outside. Davids followed with his friend in tow. I walked off to the side away from the entrance and turned to face them.

It was at this point that Tim appeared. 'Come on man, take it easy,' he said. 'It ain't worth it.'

Davids started talking to his buddy in Dutch, who in turn addressed Tim. 'Look, we don't want any trouble,' he said, 'but you have a security guard here abusing guests. Where's the manager? We'd like to make a complaint.'

Oscar the night duty manager had worked security himself and was sympathetic to the particular stresses and problems we had to deal with. He came over to talk to me, heard my version of events, and left it at that. I later apologized to Davids and his girlfriend.

In the wee small hours it was a regular occurrence to see women come and go. It didn't take a genius to work out that they were escorts and were going up to rooms to visit clients. I asked Oscar about it, about whether we should be trying to stop the practice, and he told me to just leave it. One night I engaged one of the girls in conversation just as she was leaving. Her name was Caroline, I recall. Originally from Virginia, she'd moved to LA five years ago to try and make a career as an actress and model.

With so many like her competing for the same opportunities, she found things tough going financially after a couple of years, which is why she decided to start working as an escort. What about going home? I asked. She replied that LA was her home now, and that anyway she couldn't make the kind of money she was making back there.

One night an incident occurred that illustrated just how dangerous this particular business can be. I received a call over the radio from reception that one of the guests had reported there was an intruder in his room and needed urgent assistance. I was on one of the upper floors when I received the message and immediately began heading down to the room in question. I arrived at the same time as Oscar. I knocked and moments later the door swung open.

The guy on the other side was huge, I mean really huge, as was his buddy, who was pacing up and down in the room, having to stoop lest his head hit the ceiling. Lying in the bed was the hotel guest. It turned out he'd booked an escort over the phone, only to change his mind and refuse to pay a cancellation fee when she arrived. The girl left and a few minutes later the two goons standing before me showed up to collect. It was then that the guest contacted reception.

This was a tricky situation. On the one hand the guest had booked an escort and then left her high and dry when she arrived. Add to that he was arrogant and transparently an arsehole with his attitude towards the woman in question, and it was hard to feel any sympathy. But regardless, as a guest, his safety and protection was the responsibility of the hotel. This meant we couldn't just allow him to be forced to part with money as these two goons were demanding.

Oscar as night duty manager did most of the talking. If it kicked off I didn't hold out much hope of our chances. Consequently, I spent a nervous five minutes standing in the background praying it didn't while Oscar read these two circus freaks the riot act, hoping they would see sense and leave without trouble. Eventually and thankfully they did, persuaded no doubt by Oscar threatening to get the cops involved. I was sure the sound my heart was making as it pumped the adrenalin through my veins could be heard down at reception as they departed the scene.

Ultimately, though, the nature of the job at the Mondrian and the clientele at the Skybar finally got the better of me. Weekend after weekend dealing with so many selfish, vain, arrogant people - of being showered with verbal abuse by men and women alike for failing to treat them with the deference and respect they felt they deserved - all contributed to my reaction when I found myself confronted with an arsehole in the shape of a well-connected Hollywood agent I'll call Geoff.

He came in one Thursday, generally a quiet night, with the cast and crew of a then-popular reality TV show. There were about thirty or forty of them, and they were in the mood to celebrate the end of that season's production schedule. The hotel management had given them prior permission to film in the bar. What they didn't do was inform us. Consequently, when Sean, who was on duty alongside me, spotted a girl from the group filming in the bar he approached and politely but firmly instructed her to stop, precisely as he was supposed to and as I had when Edgar Davids' girlfriend had been filming guests in the reception a couple of weeks prior.

It was now that this guy Geoff intervened, shouting that he was going to speak to the management and have Sean fired. He was a big man, around six-four with the dimensions to match, and so when he passed me at the entrance on his way out to reception, gesticulating and shouting the odds at Sean, who was following in his wake trying to calm him down, I made sure to keep an eye on things out in the foyer. This I was able to do by standing by the glass doors that separated the bar and restaurant area from the rest of the hotel.

From this vantage point I watched Geoff remonstrate with the staff at reception. When he physically pushed Sean aside I went out in case things degenerated further, taking up position in the foyer a discreet distance away. By this point he was shouting threats and insults like a man who'd lost it. It was while he was in the midst of this rant that he happened to look round and our eyes locked.

'What the fuck are you looking at?' he called over.

I looked away at first, hoping to avoid confrontation. But he kept on. 'That's it, look away. You're nothing but a fuckin' pussy.' A lot of people were tuning in, staff and guests alike. 'Yeah, look at ya,' he went on. 'You ain't shit and neither is this hotel!'

My opportunity arrived when he turned away from me to resume shouting at the girl on reception. I closed the distance, took him down from behind by the hair and began dragging him round the foyer. The place erupted, staff and guests screaming, people running to get out of the way. I was kicking and punching him as I dragged him across the floor. Sean was shouting at me to stop. I ignored him. This wasn't just about this arsehole, it was about every arsehole I'd come into contact with in my brief time working security at the Mondrian Hotel and Skybar on Sunset Boulevard.

It only lasted a few seconds before Big Stu appeared and pulled me off. Geoff stood up, disheveled and out of breath. Cowering behind Stu, humiliated and shaken, he glared at me. Seconds later he snapped himself out of his catatonic state, marched over to reception and demanded that somebody call the cops. This is the point at which I realized I had myself a problem. The police in this part of the world took assault seriously – in fact so seriously that unless I could prove I'd acted in self-defence, I was looking at the very real possibility of being arrested. Geoff knew it too. Satisfied now the cops were on their way, he was busy walking around collecting witnesses intent on ensuring my demise.

Fifteen minutes later two LA Sheriff's Department patrol cars pulled up outside. There were four of them, big guys who by their appearance and demeanour were ready for anything. Any one of them could have kicked my cunt in.

I went outside to talk to them, as did Geoff, who went straight into a diatribe about having been attacked without provocation by a member of hotel security - me. The cops separated us and took statements. I told the officer taking mine that I only hit him after he threatened me first. I judged that he was about to lash out. Given that he's a big man I decided to strike first and ask questions later. After all, I asserted politely, in this I was only following the same first-strike policy as the US government.

Just as he said he would, Sean corroborated my version of events. Combined with the fact there was no visible damage to either myself or my adversary by way of injuries, this led the cops to the conclusion that what took place was mutual combat.

Therefore no charges would be brought.

Geoff went nuts when he heard this, ranting and raving as he stormed off into the night. Meanwhile, I sauntered back into the hotel. At Oscar's behest I made my way straight to the security office, punched out my timecard and left.

Walking along Sunset Boulevard in the direction of Hollywood, neon lights marking the contours of this world famous valley of decadence and hedonism, I felt good about things. In my mind I'd just stood up for the little guy - the valets and the cleaners, the bellhops and the dishwashers - all those who work the menial, shitty jobs and spend their lives taking it from the Geoffs of this world.

I stopped off at supermarket and picked up a bottle of cheap wine. Back at the apartment, I uncorked it and poured out a large glass. Sitting myself down on the ripped, plastic armchair I'd purchased for twenty bucks at a thrift store in East LA, I sipped the wine and contemplated events. Here I was, 6000 miles from home and three months into my quest for glory. I was that close to the dream I could taste it. All I had to do was stay the course and it would all go according to plan. Don't take any shit, that's the secret in this town. People respect people who respect themselves.

I took another sip of the wine.

Yep, you really showed that prick tonight, J.

Another sip.

No doubt about it, you're a fucking hero.

Approaching the hotel the next again night for work as usual, I was stopped in my tracks by the sight of Albert and the general manager standing outside with anxious expressions on their faces. Something was up. As soon as I reached them the manager informed me that I was not allowed on the premises and that my employment was being terminated with immediate effect. Geoff's lawyer had been in contact with the hotel about initiating a civil action.

'The CCTV clearly shows you walking over and taking him from behind,' he told me. 'There's nothing in the footage - nothing at all - to suggest you were acting in self-defence.'

He ended by informing me that my final paycheque would be sent out in the mail. Then he about turned and walked back into the hotel. As soon as he was gone, Albert walked me up to the corner of Sunset Boulevard, which as usual was crawling with traffic.

'Listen to me,' he said. 'You're gonna hafta learn something quick if you're gonna survive in LA. Takin' shit in this town's an art. Assholes like Geoff are on every corner. You can't change that. Nor can you change the rules. All you can do is play em better than the next fuckin' guy. That's the only way you'll make it in this mothafucka.'

We reached the end of the street. 'Okay, Scotsman,' Albert said as he clasped my hand and shook it. 'Nice working with ya. Remember what I said now. Be smart, keep your dick in your pants, an' fly straight.'

He turned and walked towards the hotel. I stood watching him until he disappeared inside. The valets were running back and forth in their cream uniforms as luxury car after luxury car pulled up at the main entrance to disgorge their rich cargo.

Shuffling along Sunset on the way back to the apartment, my swagger of the previous night was absent. I was back to where I started - no job, no income, and no prospects with the rent due at the end of the month. The walk home seemed longer than it had the night before. On the way, Albert's words kept replaying inside my head: 'Taking shit in this town's an art.'

5

It was shortly thereafter that I visited the offices of Central Casting to sign up to work as an extra.

Dave, the young Clint Eastwood lookalike I mentioned earlier who worked as a doorman at the Skybar, had schooled me about extra work when I'd brought the subject up one night when we were working together. From him I learned that no serious actor would lower themselves to extra work. To do so would be to end your career before it began. In fact, such was the passion of his denunciation when it came to working as an extra, you would have been forgiven for thinking it was akin to the commission of some heinous crime.

Given that I did not harbour any serious acting ambitions, I concluded that none of Dave's reasons for rejecting extra work applied to me. Also, the experience of being on set watching how a movie or a television show is put together I felt would be invaluable for an aspiring writer. Perhaps it might even provide an opportunity to make some useful contacts. Anyway, the bottom line was I had no choice; I needed work, any work, to pay the bills, and I was in no position to be fussy. With this in mind, I decided it was time to get myself a car with the last of my savings. Big Stu came to the fore here. He drove a Chevy Caprice, a big gas-guzzling machine that was low on aesthetic beauty but high on reliability – at least according to Stu. More crucially you could pick one up relatively cheap. Stu spent a week helping me find one, which we did finally did in Pasadena through a newspaper ad. He drove me over to take a look. After getting the owner to lower the price a little, I decided to take it. It was battleship grey with a black canvas roof that was ripped and torn. But it had a good engine and was big and spacious inside. While I may have been able to manage without a car whilst working at the Mondrian, just a half hour walk or ten-minute bus journey from my apartment, working full time as an extra would involve travelling all over LA, whether to one of the various studio lots or on location. This meant a car was essential if I was going to stand any chance of making a living.

In this I wasn't wrong, as during the initial weeks of my new found career I was afforded a glimpse of LA all the way from downtown, where the poverty and deprivation is extreme, to Santa Monica and Malibu, where wealth and health march hand in hand. The differences could be so stark from location to location it often felt as if I were travelling between different countries rather than parts of the same county.

Day in day out I would pack my bag with my wardrobe selection (as a non-union extra it was mandatory to wear one and bring three changes of wardrobe to every job), and leave it just inside the door of the apartment to save me carrying it all the way down to the parking garage. Then, invariably running late, I would complete the walk down the street and across Hollywood Boulevard to the parking garage quick-style, passing on the way the gang members selling crack on the corner and the homeless crackheads who lived in the alley bordering the parking garage. I would reach the car, jump in, and drive back up to the apartment building. There I would double park, jump out and rush as fast as I could into the building and along the hall to my apartment, where I would quickly open the door, grab my bag, lock the door, and rush back out in order to return to the car before I got hit with a ticket. I didn't always succeed.

Much of the time when I wasn't working - one of the perks of being an extra was the possibility of working just a few hours before being 'wrapped' if you were only in one or two scenes - I usually spent at the computer working on a new screenplay or rewriting an old one; either that or getting my regular endorphin fix with a run through Runyon Canyon or a workout at the gym.

Runyon is a large park located just a ten walk north of Sycamore Avenue at the eastern end of the Santa Monica

Mountains. The story goes it had been estate of Errol Flynn, who left it to the city after he died. I never did find out if the story was true or not, but as a natural sanctuary from the noise and chaos of the city Runyon Canyon was unsurpassed. You never saw many people out there in the middle of the day, especially during the summer months when temperatures often reached the high eighties and above. And if you did they'd be walking at an easy pace. Come evening, though, the place was packed with people out walking, jogging or just enjoying the bucolic surroundings. Morning, noon, or night it was an antidote to the stress of trying to survive and find your way in the madness that is LA. Nights, standing at the top and watching the sun go down over a red sky stretching as far as the eye could see, the city unfolding below like a white blanket, something always stirred inside. As for early mornings, with the air fresh and the temperature cool, I never failed to come away feeling cleansed and reborn.

Once or twice a week, I substituted Runyon Canyon for workouts at the Wildcard Boxing Club on the rundown corner of Santa Monica and Vine. Wildcard was a sanctuary of a different sort. Here men and women congregated to push and challenge themselves in the sport of boxing. Owned by Freddie Roach, one-time top ten professional lightweight before rising to become one of the most respected trainers in the sport, the gym made up with energy and spirit what it lacked in décor and amenities. It was no place for the faint-hearted or those of a sensitive disposition. It was hard, and if you wanted to be accepted you were expected to put some work in.

The characters who frequented Wildcard is too long to recount, but I respected them all. World champions and top contenders trained there every day, interspersed with the odd familiar face from the world of film and television, Hollywood execs, and various others all looking to keep fit. In addition old-timers, hustlers, and ordinary fans of the sport would come to Wildcard just to watch the pros train, taking up position on the chairs that were lined up against the wall as you walked in. The smell of sweat and leather dominated, as did the sounds of bags being pummelled, ropes whipping the hard floor in the far corner that was designated for skipping, the sharp gunshot of pads being punched, and the regular pierce of the buzzer signifying the start and end of each round. Above it all were the harsh voices of grizzled trainers shouting instructions, demanding more effort, and/or lending encouragement to fighters as they dug deep in their quest for greatness.

The casualties of a sport that takes everything and all too often offers little in return were also in evidence, men who'd spent their best years in the ring without tasting glory or money and were now paying the price in slurred speech and an unsteady gait. For them the gym continued to be the one place where they were still respected and belonged in an increasingly unsympathetic world.

The Hollywood types, I always felt, were drawn to the spartan surroundings and atmosphere as an antidote to the bullshit that dominated the status-driven environment they were part of on the other side of the door. To watch one of them being shouted at and verbally abused by one of the trainers, while being put through their paces on the pads, was like watching someone being purified with pain for all the abuse they themselves doled out to others in their professional lives. Carl Jung would have had a field day.

I remember at the gym one day being distracted from by the sound of somebody screaming. I stopped to look. In the ring a tiny guy I'd never seen before was shadowboxing. He was Filipino, nothing much to look at it has to be said, but he was fast. In fact he was so fast his hands moved in a blur. He had this crazed look on his face too, born of desperation it seemed to me. There were many like that at Wildcard, guys who'd come from nothing and looked on boxing as their salvation. But I'd never seen anything like the intensity I saw on this skinny Filipino's face. That said, despite his speed and intensity, he looked too scrawny to have any chance of making it. Like most who came through here the poor kid would probably be on a flight home to obscurity in a few months time, nothing to show for the experience apart from bruises and a broken bank account. Somebody told me later his name was Manny Pacquiao.

I sparred at the gym only when I felt I had to. In any boxing gym, no matter how hard you try to resist, the pull of the ring eventually proves too strong. A feeling of having to spar in order to attain and maintain the respect of your peers is always present. Nothing is ever said because nothing has to. But it's there nonetheless, that pressure, hanging over you like an incubus.

I worked (fighters commonly referred to sparring as work) with this huge bear of a Russian once. He trained in the evenings, when the gym was turned into an outpost of the former Soviet Union - Armenians, Russians, Azerbaijanis, etc. - and English became a foreign language. Anyway, due to my erratic work schedule, occasionally I could only make it to the gym in the evening. It was on one such evening that I first encountered Jimmy, the name this monster went by, when he approached as I was in the middle of hitting one of the heavy bags.

'You…you want to work with me?' he asked me in a heavy Russian accent. I stopped and looked at him, at the size of him, standing there in a vest with his massive head perched on top of equally massive shoulders. 'Don't worry about it,' he continued, reading my hesitation, 'I go easy with you. We just work to the body.'

In that moment fear gave way to embarrassment at the suggestion I was in any way afraid. Of course, I *was* afraid, everyone who steps through the ropes is. The secret is not to show it. But this guy had just told me that I was showing him my fear and the resulting slight could not go unanswered.

'Okay, let's go,' I said, in a voice designed to project an image of steel and determination in place of the fear and doubt with which I'd originally met the challenge. We climbed through the ropes into a ring already occupied by two or three people who were shadowboxing. But as soon as they saw that we were about to spar they made way in accordance with the unwritten rule that sparring came before every other activity in the gym.

As we were only going to the body there was no need to put on protective headgear, which I hated wearing anyway as it was uncomfortable and slowed you down - not that I was fast to begin with. Jimmy was pacing back and forth on the opposite side of the ring as we waited for the buzzer to sound, marking the start of a fresh three-minute round.

I suddenly became aware of the small audience that had gathered to watch, which only added to the pressure not to mention trepidation. This was not going to be fun, I could tell. Jimmy could bang with the best of them and an expression of grim determination on his face revealed that he'd lied when he said he would go easy. On the contrary, this bastard was set on taking me out.

The buzzer went and we met in the middle of the ring, each with our arms covering our torsos for protection. I ventured a couple of jabs. Each rebounded harmlessly off his gloves. He stayed in front of me, eyes staring a hole through my midsection in anticipation of the damage he meant to inflict. Beginning to panic, I began teeing off with lefts and rights, straight punches rather than hooks or uppercuts, in a desperate effort to back him up. But my punches were having little effect and he was able to walk through them. My strength and confidence proceeded to drain away.

We'd been going for half a round and Jimmy was still to throw a punch. Some of his mates were shouting instructions to him in Russian. I had no idea what they were saying but I could tell they were enjoying this, eagerly anticipating my destruction. Then it happened. Suddenly, he let loose with a volley of hooks and uppercuts. My arms were crossed over my body as a protective shield and took most of them. I was destined to have welts and bruises over the entire length of each for days afterwards.

But at that moment this was the least of my problems, because one of Jimmy's uppercuts sneaked through and got me in the solar plexus. I lurched forward in response, a curtain of pain dropping over my brain as I grabbed and forced him back onto the ropes.

'Are you all right?!' I shouted at him, in a vain but desperate attempt to buy myself time, hoping in my wildest dreams that he would say no and stop. It was a stupid question. Of course he was all right. He was in the middle of taking me apart. He couldn't have been more all right.

By the end of the third I was done in, desperate for the buzzer to sound the end of the round before he cut me in half with more crushing body shots. Finally, thankfully, it sounded. I almost fell out of the ring, I was that desperate to get out of there. By the time I reached the car I was about ready to collapse.

From then on I made sure to avoid the gym in the evenings.

Extra work was keeping me busy during this period. Working non-union for minimum wage I was out five days a week every week; sometimes more if I opted to work an additional day or two over the weekend. I couldn't afford to work any less than five days, the money was so bad. Talking to people who were in the union (Screen Actors Guild) would fill me with envy. Their base rate was more than double that of their non-union counterparts. But it was their overtime rate that really made the difference, allowing them to make hundreds in a single day depending on how long they were on set. They also got meal penalties (a set amount if the production continued shooting over union stipulated breaks for meals), a wardrobe allowance for bringing a choice of outfits to set, mileage (a subsidy to cover fuel costs if they had to travel over a certain distance to an outside location), and various other little perks in their pay and conditions. There was also the important fact that in order to be eligible to take principle parts or book commercials you had to be in the union as well. The basic SAG rate for lines on a TV show or a movie at the time was 750 bucks a day. On commercials, with residuals, the sky was the limit. This is why commercial work was the most sought after and why as a result it was almost impossible to get.

In my early thirties and over six feet in height, I was commonly booked to work as a cop, detective, soldier, doctor, or 'business type'. I hated it when I was booked to be a cop or soldier, as it entailed having to wear a uniform and getting changed in one of the tiny changing cubicles allocated for the extras in the production trailer. If you were working a scene or scenes with a lot of extras you literally had to force your way forward to get into one of these cubicles. And when you did you had to share the space with two or three others. Moreover, the uniforms they gave you were not devised with comfort in mind, especially the LAPD uniform, which was made of a coarse, heavy material. They also typically insisted that you wear a bulletproof vest underneath in the interests of authenticity. In LA, with the weather as hot as it is, anytime you were booked to work as a cop you were guaranteed an uncomfortable experience. The wardrobe department who allocated you the uniform added to your stress levels with their stipulation that everything had to be handed back exactly the way it had been handed out. This meant putting the uniform back on the wire hanger exactly as they wanted it, with the cap, tie, and shoes all affixed in the proper manner. If it wasn't, they would return it to you and make you do it again. At the end of a long day on set, when all you wanted to do was get in your car and get out of there, this was the last thing you needed.

Despite the drawbacks, I had no choice but to persevere if I wanted to survive. It was easier said than done, especially when the disrespect and derision emanating from members of the crew and production staff on some sets towards the extras was in your face. Some extras, it has to be said, didn't do themselves any favours. The nature of the work, the accessibility and low pay, made it inevitable that a fair amount of misfits would be attracted to it. You occasionally came across them, and whenever you did you tried your utmost to keep a safe distance. If I found myself confronted by one I would extricate myself as painlessly and quickly as I could, usually by excusing myself to go to the bathroom. The places to watch out were the craft service table and extras-holding. During the long periods of hanging around between shots, I preferred to sit alone and read a book rather than pass the time in banal conversation with the others. It was an approach designed to preserve my sanity, but at the same time one that didn't win me many friends.

The first big production I worked on as an extra was the action movie *Swordfish,* starring John Travolta, Halle Berry, Hugh Jackman, and the one and only Vinnie Jones, whose emergence as a Hollywood actor proved that in this business even a blind chicken gets a piece of corn sometimes. I was booked to work it in a big nightclub scene along with a couple of hundred of others. It was a major production with a big budget and the extras were fitted with their outfits in advance. The costume warehouse I had to report to was located in Burbank and I drove out there one sunny afternoon. Some felt that being cast as an extra in a big-budget movie that required you to be costume-fitted in advance meant something. In truth all it meant was losing a day's regular pay of a measly fifty bucks for the even more measly fifteen you got for the fitting.

It took me a while to find the place, even with the help of my Thomas Guide (LA street guide and indispensable tool for an extra working over such a vast geographical area as Los Angeles County). But I was useless at reading maps, my sense of direction was awful, and more often than not I found places by stumbling upon them by accident. Finally, after driving past the place two or three times, I managed to locate it. I pulled in, got out and walked in the main entrance, only to be told by the girl at reception that the fitting was taking place all the way round the back of the building. I got back in my Chevy and drove down the side of the place, which was huge, until I reached the end and turned right into a large parking lot. The entire length of the building at the back was made up of loading bays, the same as you'd find at any large warehouse or supply depot. Above one was sign that said "Swordfish". I parked opposite and headed over.

Just inside the loading bay, which you reached by climbing a set of stairs, a youngish guy was seated behind a desk with vouchers laid out in neat piles in front of him: green for nonunion and white for union.

'Uh … hello. I'm here for the fitting.' I gave him my name.

'Union or non?'

I'd been asked this question a hundred times by now. It was the first question you were asked on every set when you arrived to check-in and it never failed to make me feel like a deadbeat.

'Non.'

He ran his finger down a long list of names on a white sheet of paper spread out on the desk in front of him until he came to my name.

'You were meant to be here an hour ago.'

'Yeah, I'm sorry about that. I had trouble finding the place. I'm not …'

'Don't worry about it. Here's your voucher. Take a seat, fill it in, somebody'll call ya through to be fitted.'

'Okay. Uh … could I borrow a pen?'

'You didn't bring a pen?'

'No … well … I left in a rush and …'

He let out a sigh. 'Here. Remember to give it back.'

I walked over to a row of red, plastic chairs, a few of which were occupied by others who were also there to be fitted. There were a few attractive-looking girls among them, only to be expected given it was a nightclub scene we were booked to work.

There were also three or four guys, all of them young and wannabe-cool, talking among each other. They were posturing and posing for the benefit of the girls, who for the most part weren't paying them any attention.

'Hey, dude,' one of the guys called out to me in a voice loud enough for everyone to hear.

I looked up at him.

'You know who you look like?'

'No…who?' I said, already feeling my face flush red with embarrassment, both for him and for me.

'Matthew Perry.'

'Really?'

'You should find out who books Friends at Central and see if he needs a stand-in.'

'I'm sure he's already got it covered,' I said, hoping that would be the end of it.

'Hey, I like your accent,' one of the girls interjected. 'Where are you from?'

'Scotland.'

'I like it. It's cute.'

I said nothing.

'How long have you been in LA?'

By now everyone was listening in.

'Six months,' I replied.

'How d'ya like it?'

'Good.'

'Oh, I'd love to visit Scatland. So green.'

'Hey, man, wasn't Braveheart set in Scatland?'

'Yes.'

'Oh, man, that's a great fuckin' movie.'

'Yes.'

'So you come out here for acting?'

'No, writing.'

'You write scripts?'

'Yes.'

'What kinda stuff d'ya write?'

'I'm working on a script myself right now,' one of the other guys said. 'It's an action movie ... lotsa shit being blown up. I'm gonna do what Affleck and Damon did with their script and star in it myself.'

'You could make it as an actor with your accent, you know that?' the girl said.

I didn't have an answer to that and sitting there with the sweat pouring down my back all I wanted to do was leave. But just as I was seriously contemplating doing exactly that a man appeared and called my name to be fitted.

The fitting consisted of me trying on various outfits, selected by the people doing the fitting, until they decided on one. A polaroid was taken of me in the outfit in question - in this case a very tight-fitting, outrageously-patterned silk shirt, blue in colour, and a pair of dark brown flared trousers with brown ankle boots - after which I was free to leave. I walked out of there desperate to get back to the car and hasten my return to the relative sanity of Hollywood.

I opened the door, got behind the wheel, inserted the key in the ignition and turned.

Nothing happened.

I tried it again.

Again, nothing happened.

The engine was completely dead.

I rode home in a tow truck. It cost me 300 bucks. Things were going from bad to worse.

The scene I was booked to work in was scheduled to be shot over three days at a disused warehouse deep in the heart of downtown Los Angeles. Armed with the directions provided by Central Casting and my trusty Thomas Guide, I jumped into the car and headed along the 101 Freeway South early on the morning of the first day. It was fortunate that the call-time was seven in the morning, as it meant that the traffic on the 101 was still free-flowing. In my time I would lose count of the number of hours spent sitting in traffic on either the 101 or the 405 freeways with the sun beating down and the clothes sticking to my back in a car with no air-con, feeling utterly miserable.

But as I said, on this particular occasion the drive downtown was comfortable and smooth.

After taking the requisite exit, followed by the various streets as directed, I finally pulled into the parking lot designated for crew parking. As they were providing the wardrobe, all I had with me was a small bag containing a couple of snacks, water, and some reading material. I parked, grabbed my stuff, and walked to one of the three shuttle vans waiting to ferry the extras to the location. I climbed in via the side door and squeezed my way over to one of the vacant seats at the back. Two or three more people got on just after me and then the van took off for the set.

Ten minutes later we arrived outside a huge marquee that had been set up adjacent to the usual array of production trailers, catering trucks, and various crew trucks, a separate one for each department - camera, sound, property, wardrobe, lighting and so on. As on any big movie production, it was a scene of mayhem and madness. Groups of extras were milling around, being herded here and there by a small army of PAs and ADs.

Clutching my bag, I followed the others who'd come in on the same shuttle van in the direction of the marquee. Inside, row after row of long tables and plastic chairs were set up, occupied by a sea of people. If anyone ever needed any confirmation about the sheer number of people working as extras in Hollywood, all they have to do is visit any big movie set, take in the number of extras on it, and multiply that number by the plethora of movies and TV shows that are in production in LA on any given day.

I joined one of the three long lines of extras set up in front of the tables where three members of the production staff were sitting checking us all in and dishing out vouchers. Once we'd checked in we were instructed to make for the wardrobe trailer parked just outside to get our outfits. This meant another wait in a long line. I was still tired from the early start and the activity and noise created by so many people thrown together jarred the senses. I resolved to get my wardrobe, change quickly, and find a quiet corner where I could settle down in peace and quiet with a book.

It came my turn and I handed my voucher over to one of the three harassed wardrobe girls, who immediately retreated into the deep recesses of the trailer, stacked end to end with clothes. She returned seconds later with my outfit, handing it over after first ripping off the bottom copy of my voucher to keep until the outfit had been returned at the end of the day's shooting. She then pointed me in the direction of another marquee that had been set up as the changing room. There were two – one male and one female. The male one was packed with hardly enough room to swing the proverbial cat. There was little conversation or banter flowing. It was too early and most of us hadn't had any breakfast. Grabbing some from the catering truck before there was none left was a priority.

Twenty minutes or so later, carrying my plastic tray on top of which sat a paper plate filled with food and the obligatory cup of coffee in a styrofoam cup, I found a vacant space at one of the long tables and started to eat. Soon I was joined at the table by others, none of whom I'd set eyes on or met before. On a movie set among extras the conventional barriers that normally separate contact with strangers are swiftly removed on the understanding that everybody's in the same boat, forced to share the same space for how many hours you're there. As a result, no sooner had the table filled up than the conversation started to flow, everybody's mood lifting in line with the hot food that was hitting our stomachs.

When we were finally called to set, escorted in by one of the many PAs in batches of ten, there was a buzz of excitement.

Animated conversations were taking place as the prospect of working on a movie in proximity to the likes of John Travolta and Halle Berry. The magic was doing its work.

The entire floor of a disused warehouse had been converted into a vast, upscale nightclub in Prague, complete with a bar, tables and chairs, along with the requisite fittings. The extras had been specially fitted in trendy outfits, as befitted the décor and style of the set, and all this for just three days of shooting a scene that in the finished movie would last all of five minutes onscreen. I was placed as far away from the action as it was possible to be, standing at a table in the opposite corner where I was directed to interact with the people who were sat at the table. Standing there waiting (on a movie or TV set you do more waiting than anything else), I passed the time chatting. Suddenly, one of the girls I was talking to looked behind me. Instinctively, I turned to look at what she was looking at only to be confronted by John Travolta standing no more than five feet away. He couldn't help but notice a 6'2" extra swivelling round to look at him. I did the only thing I could do under the circumstances and hit him with a thumbs up. Travolta gave me a thumbs up in return before walking on in the direction of the set.

Then Halle Berry appeared, accompanied by the obligatory personal assistant and bodyguard. As with Travolta, when she appeared you could feel the atmosphere in the place change. It became heightened, more intense, with people staring as she moved through and among them. While objectively you know that famous people are just as human as anyone else, in possession of the same frailties, weaknesses etc., it is easy to fall into the trap of believing that they are somehow special, possessed of super human qualities that set them apart from the rest of humanity. They are famous, their faces known throughout the world, with their every move, gesture and word venerated, pored over and dissected. Through this exposure there isn't a corner of the world where they aren't recognized and it's this realization that colours our perception of them. Here on this movie set everybody was studying John Travolta and Halle Berry as if trying to work out what it was they had that made them so special. They were desperate to find out because they wanted to be just like them - rich, famous and fawned over.

6

So, yes, I was scheduled to work three days on the movie *Swordfish*. But after that first day destiny took me in a different direction altogether and I never made it back for the other two.

Living in the heart of Hollywood, I was in walking distance of an assortment of nightclubs, bars, restaurants, and strip clubs. Every Thursday, Friday and Saturday night the boulevard would be jam-packed with vehicles of every description. All the way along this weekly procession of souped-up trucks, sports cars and stretch limos, music blasted from stereo systems and guys and girls screamed to one another out of open windows. It was a scene of chaos and noise that assaulted the senses and on weekend nights, having to negotiate these crowds and this traffic on the way home, just getting back to the apartment and being able to shut the door was accompanied by relief.

But on this particular night, having completed my first day as an extra on a major movie, I decided to venture out for a drink.

Located at the top of La Brea, adjacent to the parking garage where I paid a monthly fee to park my car, was one of the more popular nightclubs in Hollywood, the euphemistically named Garden of Eden. Whenever I walked past the place after parking the car late at night, there was always a large crowd waiting outside trying to get in.

Tonight, though, instead of walking past, I was intent on going in to see what all the fuss was about. I parked the car, got back to the apartment, threw some food down my neck, jumped in the shower, and quickly got changed. It had just gone past ten and the club would just be opening. Thus it was the perfect time to gain entry, as most people would arrive between 11 and 12 to create a scene of mayhem outside the likes of which old Charlie Darwin would have been able to call upon in support of his theory of the survival of the fittest.

The challenge would be talking my way past the promoter behind the rope. Vested within him was the power to make or ruin the night of the hundreds who flocked to this establishment from far and wide. It is no accident that club promoters in Hollywood are considered minor celebrities in their own right, especially those that run and work the more popular club nights.

You see them standing on the other side of that ubiquitous velvet rope, typically dressed up to the nines, cool and confident as they bask in their all-powerful status. Everyone does their utmost to win their favour, hoping to be admitted into the bar or club in question, in the process outdoing themselves in the art of supplication. But this should come as no surprise, not when you consider that in the rarefied environs of Hollywood an individual's intrinsic worth is measured by whether or not they belong.

The famous and the well-connected never have a problem and swagger up to the front of the line and continue on through the rope, held open for them by the promoter, without as much as a second's hesitation. Those occupying the second tier of importance might have to wait a few minutes before they too are allowed in; and so on in descending order of status. If you aren't on the guest list, or don't know the promoter, you're reduced to trying to bluff your way in, usually by dropping an important name or two; either that or offering the promoter a handsome bribe, which in the business is referred to as a 'tip'. At the more in-demand places sometimes even this isn't enough, as some promoters will refuse a tip from just anyone, more concerned with maintaining the club's reputation by keeping out the riff-raff than they are in lining their own pocket with a few extra bucks.

Sad but true, the overwhelming majority of mere mortals who venture out to sample the Hollywood club scene are destined for long night of standing patiently in line outside hoping that patience and humility might eventually pay off. But in this part of the world, where self-assertion and ego reigns, patience and humility describe weakness rather than virtue. Here the meek absolutely and definitely do not inherit the earth.

What this means is that a night out in Hollywood is fraught with all sorts of challenges, not least to ensure that you come through the other side with your self-esteem, self-respect, and humanity intact.

But even though I didn't know anybody and was a complete nobody when it came to that invisible but no less fixed totem pole of success and status, I did have in my possession the security ID badge from my time working at the Mondrian Hotel. I'd retained it after being fired and now was the time to find out if it was worth holding on to. So I grabbed my wallet, the ID badge, and made my way down the street to the club.

I arrived outside five minutes later to find I'd been correct in choosing to get there early. It was still relatively quiet and I was able to approach the promoter behind the rope without having to wait in a line; or, to be more accurate, amid a large, seething crowd of desperate humanity.

'Hey,' the promoter said on seeing me approach. 'Can I help you with something?'

He was about my age, maybe a couple of years younger, and you could tell by the way he carried himself - not too cocky like some promoters, but confident and assertively polite - that he knew his business.

'How are you doing?' I said. 'I work security at the Skybar over at the Mondrian. It's my night off. I was wondering if there was any chance of getting in tonight?'

'You work security at the Skybar?' the promoter said, his face betraying the fact I'd piqued his interest. 'I know the guys over there. When did you start?'

'A few months ago. Here's my ID.'

He examined it up close for a few long moments.

'Okay ... my name's Gary. I promote a club here Thursdays

and Fridays. You're welcome to come down anytime.' He stamped my hand, opened the rope, and as I walked through he turned to the big bouncer standing by the door and called out, 'Straight through.'

I turned back, said thanks, and walked in, the door kindly being held open by the bouncer. It was the perfect start to the night and I made my way straight to the bar, where I ordered a cool glass of wine. This society is all about self-promotion, it came to me as I took my first sip, and rewarded are those who are prepared to be bold.

Within an hour the place was packed, making it impossible to walk through without having to negotiate and squeeze past the throng of people who filled every foot of space. As in all clubs, the dance floor was the main focus, exerting a magnetic pull. I moved up to the mezzanine level via the steps that lay to the right. Here there was another bar, in addition to the club's VIP lounge, demarcated by the ubiquitous velvet rope and another very large bouncer. I went to the bar, got myself another glass of wine, and stood watching the action unfold from a safe distance. I became aware of a tall blonde in the VIP area over to my right. She was dancing by herself, sipping champagne from a glass that she periodically lifted from the table beside her. She was so hot it was hard to do anything else except stare, and at that moment I was just one of four or five guys dotted around doing exactly that. I continued watching her for a minute or so before returning my focus to the dance floor, resigned to the fact she was out of my league. Just moments later I felt a tap on my shoulder. I turned. It was her.

'Would you like to join me?' she said, revealing in the process a European accent that upon hearing for the first time I guessed was German but turned out to be Dutch. It took me a few moments to regroup from the surprise. By that time she'd grabbed my hand and was leading me over to the VIP lounge, the bouncer opening the rope to let us through. The gods were with me.

She led me over to her table and poured me out a glass of champagne. Introducing herself as Melina, she said she was here with a group of friends who were in town for a couple of weeks. They were visiting from Amsterdam, her home town. I sipped the champagne still trying to digest the suddenness with which this woman had just crashed into my life.

I didn't get a chance to think about it for long, because no sooner had I taken two sips of champagne than she was grabbing my hand again and leading me from the VIP area out to the smoking patio. Here her friends were congregated, laughing and drinking. Melina, or Mel as she preferred to be called, introduced me. They were all very friendly - in fact so friendly that all of a sudden somebody was handing me a bong. Though not a smoker of marijuana or anything else for that matter, for some reason it seemed the perfect time and place to start and so without a moment's hesitation I placed the end to my mouth, waited until somebody lit the other end, and inhaled. I started to cough at the same time as my head left my shoulders and began floating upwards.

The next couple of hours passed in a blur. In fact when the music stopped and the lights came up, I had to check the time to make sure the management weren't shutting the place early.

'Everyone is coming back to my house for drinks,' Mel said. 'Would you like to come?' I was so drunk and stoned that words were impossible to come by. Instead I made do with a nod of the head. 'Good,' she said, 'I'm glad', whereupon she leaned over and put her tongue in my mouth.

Outside people were milling around in large groups, the resulting crescendo of voices merging with the growl of engines as BMWs, Mercs, Lexuses, stretch limos and souped-up trucks of every description pulled in and out of the kerb, music booming and guys shouting at the girls in a last ditch effort to get with one, the girls laughing and shouting back.

I jumped into the back of a Merc that pulled up from nowhere, squeezing between three people I'd only just met. Mel was seated up front in the driver's seat, while sitting next to her a girl was fiddling with the volume on the sound system. We sped off on the short distance down La Brea to Sunset Boulevard, where we turned right and began heading west. Behind us another two cars filled with more people were following, forming a convoy. Mel drove while toking on the joint that was being passed around. Dance music was blasting from the sound system and both combined to make my head swirl as we travelled through a valley of neon along the Sunset Strip in what seemed like a scene ripped straight from a sci-fi movie. I had no idea where we were headed. I envisaged her living in a comfortable Westside apartment, perhaps in Brentwood or Santa Monica somewhere. But when we turned off Sunset and began heading deep into Bel Air, following a twisting climb around and up past the luxurious residences of the rich and famous, I didn't know what to think. More than that I was worried at the speed this crazy woman was taking the blind bends of a road that was swathed in darkness - one hand on the wheel, the other punching the air in rhythm to the music as the joint continued to be be passed around and everyone laughing and talking over one another.

Finally, we turned into the driveway of a large house set in spacious grounds behind a wall of trees and bushes. Surely she doesn't live here, I thought, taken aback at the palatial surroundings. We entered the house, which was massive, and everyone repaired to a large sitting room. An equally large kitchen was situated adjacent.

Mel went to the kitchen and started pouring drinks, inviting everyone to help themselves, which we did. Someone put on some music, while out of nowhere another bong appeared and was passed around. I planked myself down on one of four large leather sofas and watched the room and everyone in it spinning round in front of my eyes. Drug and drink-fuelled conversations were taking place, none of them making any sense. I'd never been so drunk or stoned and was conscious of being unable to speak properly. The words were forming in my brain as normal, but they insisted on leaving my mouth all mangled and jumbled up. I don't remember much of anything past a certain point, except the odd occasion when some guy came up and offered me a pill, which I popped without demur. By the time Mel appeared in front of me, grabbed both my hands in hers and tried to hoist me up off the couch, my legs had become detached and I limped off with her like a baby deer just left its mother's womb struggling to find its feet. By the time I'd climbed the stairs to her bedroom, doing so slowly while leaning on the banister for support, I was fit for nothing except collapsing on top of the bed in a heap with my clothes on.

Unsurprisingly then I failed to turn up for my second day as an extra on *Swordfish*. Nor did I turn up for the third. In fact over the next month or so I didn't work at all. Instead I spent my days at Mel's Bel Air mansion, lying on the couch or out on the sun deck recovering from the previous night's exertions at some club or party somewhere. Every night I was either drunk or stoned, and gone completely after a week was my self-discipline. I met each morning in a haze, while remarkably Mel would be up early to make breakfast for her 8-year-old son before taking him to school like the quintessential dedicated mother.

Quite literally she swept me off my feet. No sooner had we met than she was doing my laundry, taking me out to clubs, bars and restaurants, and paying my bills. In her massive bedroom, decorated lavishly in the style of a boudoir, we spent a lot of time in bed. She had a jacuzzi just off the bedroom, set adjacent to a large set of French windows leading out to a large balcony. On the rare nights we spent at home we would sit in the jacuzzi sharing a bottle of champagne, the French windows open as we looked out at a scene of perfect stillness. It was the only time we were alone and able to talk.

Mel's story was the stuff of fiction. A catwalk model in her twenties, during the height of the supermodel phenomenon of the eighties and early nineties, she worked at all the major fashion shows in Paris and Milan. A rich Arab saw her picture and contacted her through her agency. A woman imbued with the liberal values of the country she grew up in, rather than shy away from such an offer she agreed to meet him on a dinner date in Monaco. He flew her out there in a private jet and thereafter they were never apart. A distant cousin of the Saudis, he was extremely rich, and though already married to three women he told Mel he wanted her to be his fourth. She agreed, they were married in private in Paris, and she travelled with him to his house in Bahrain. Rather than balk at sharing her new husband with three other women, as you might expect, she loved it, especially the camaraderie she enjoyed with the other wives. When she fell pregnant her future seemed assured.

But then her husband was instructed by his family that such a union with a non-Muslim was impermissible. Forced as a consequence to choose between Mel and their newborn son or the wealth and prestige that came with being a member of a rich dynasty, he opted for the wealth and prestige.

Mel was devastated when he broke the news. But after she thought about it she accepted that in the end he had little choice. He pledged to take care of her and the boy financially, telling her he would set her up to live anywhere in the world she chose. She decided on LA because she had friends there. This and no other reason is why she ended up renting a mansion in Bel Air, living off the forty grand a month her ex gave her to look after herself and their son.

Her story left me bewildered at the fact she'd want to be with someone like me, a guy that was so broke he couldn't even afford to pay attention. It turns out she had a thing for Scottish men as a result of a previous affair with one she met in Marbella, which along with Ibiza was her favoured European destination. The guy in question was on the run from the police in the UK, she claimed. I reminded her of him, she told me, though I wasn't sure how she could equate a guy living on the lam in the Costa del Sol with one living the life of a wannabe screenwriter in Hollywood.

It didn't matter. All I knew was that suddenly I was living in a Bel Air mansion with an ex-model, spending my nights sitting in a jacuzzi drinking champagne or out at parties and nightclubs. The nightclubs and the parties I didn't need, the intimate evenings I did. My hope was that in time she would abandon the entourage of hangers-on that surrounded her, either at the house or at the bars and clubs we went to, and instead prefer the exclusive company of just one hanger-on in the shape of yours truly.

Alas, such hopes proved wishful thinking. Indeed, after just a few weeks it all started to unravel.

Every Tuesday night Mel went to a club night at a bar in Beverly Hills that was owned by Stewart Copeland, drummer with the huge and internationally famous rock band The Police back in the day. The name of the bar was Backstage and there I was introduced to a cast of characters straight out of the tragi-comedy that passes for normality in Hollywood. Ex-pop stars, actors fallen on hard times, ageing ex-models, wannabe producers - you name it, they were all there, a fraternity of failure and bitterness drowning their sorrows in booze and drugs.

Once the bar closed everyone would get in their cars and head back to Mel's for the ritual after-party. It was at the second of these gatherings after I began seeing her that I first lost the plot.

Being both attractive and rich, Mel was a prime target for the attentions of men wherever she went. Whenever we were out she drew admiring glances. When we first got involved she was honest enough to tell me that she had other guys she sometimes met up with, specifically guys she would go and visit abroad a few times each year. Rather than being repulsed by this, I was okay with it; at this point, having only just met, I looked upon our relationship as nothing more than a casual fling that could and would only last for a few weeks, if that.

But that didn't mean I would be all right with other men

coming on to her right in front of me. I wasn't that liberal or open-minded. In fact where this was concerned I was a veritable caveman; the product of an environment in which such behaviour was akin to a declaration of total war.

So as I was saying, on our second night out at *Backstage* an incident occurred that to all intents heralded the beginning of the end. At the bar I was introduced to some guy I'd never laid eyes on before. I politely shook his hand, we exchanged a few words of bullshit, and I forgot all about him. But as the night progressed I began to notice he was spending an inordinate amount of time leaning over the table deep in conversation with Mel. I wasn't unduly concerned or irritated by it initially; she was popular and knew a lot of people and we were in a large company, so it was no doubt just one of those things. I'd merely noticed it, that's all.

It was later back at the house that things erupted.

I was seated in my usual position on the couch, engaged in the usual mindless chit chat with people sitting next to me on either side. From this vantage point I had a view of the kitchen and saw the same guy trying to kiss Mel as she was pouring him and herself out a drink. She pushed him away, the two of them laughing, before they came through and set the drinks down on the large table in the centre of the room. Mel and her admirer then sat down on the floor on the other side of the table from where I was sat. He sidled up close and began whispering in her ear. Watching this, the red mist began to descend. Sitting next to me, one of Mel's friend noticed and tried to distract my attention. Too late. Without warning I brought my fist down hard on top of the table, scattering the drinks all over the place and causing everyone to jump back in fright.

'You ya bastard!' I shouted at the guy as I stood up and pointed at him across the room. The house was in disarray, everybody freaking out, with Mel jumping up and running round the table in my direction.

'Sweetie, it's all right. We're only flirting. He knows I'm with you.'

Waving her away, I marched self-righteously in the direction of the door. I walked out of the house and along the driveway to where my car was parked. Three or four other cars were blocking it in. I turned and marched back into the house, back into the sitting room, where they were all still getting over the shock of my initial outburst.

'Right! Whoever's blocking me in better get their arses ootside and move their cars now!'

I was in no state to drive but didn't care. I steered that thing down the sharp bends and twists and turns of a road that was treacherous even in daytime when taken sober. I drove all the way along Sunset Boulevard, usually crawling with cops at this time, and back to Hollywood without being pulled over. I walked into my tiny studio apartment, got undressed and flipped the light switch.

There'd been more than enough drama for one night.

Regret arrived the next morning along with the by-now-customary hangover as soon as I opened my eyes. Looking up at the ceiling fan spinning round in the centre of the tiny room in which I ate, slept, dressed, shat and worked, I pieced it all together. It was good while it lasted, but now it was over. Fuck it.

I didn't own a cellphone so couldn't be contacted when I left the apartment to head down the street for a coffee at the café I frequented. I spent an hour there contemplating the chaos of my existence, before arriving back at the apartment to a voicemail message on the phone. It was from Mel. She thought the incident last night hilarious, that I was off my head, and that she would call me as soon as she returned from her planned trip to the south of France in two weeks time. As soon as I heard her message my heart soared. I'd thought my arse was out the window but now here she was telling me all was forgiven.

But in those two weeks, returning to the life of a struggling screenwriter and a non-union extra, I began to realize there could be no future with Mel. In just the short amount of time we'd been together my self-discipline had gone awol, along with my mind. Lording it round a Bel Air mansion, being taken to parties and nightclubs by a rich ex-model may have been exciting to begin with, but now it left me feeling empty and soulless.

But then, thinking about it more, my soul could wait. As soon as she returned from her trip and got back in touch a couple of weeks later, I was over there like a shot.

Come the following Tuesday night there we were again, arriving at Backstage in Beverly Hills for the regular get-together with her friends and various hangers-on. On the basis of Oscar Wilde's dictum that 'Every saint has a past and every sinner has a future', I was hoping to be reacquainted with Mel's friends in a spirt of reconciliation and forgiveness. I was disappointed. The looks on their faces when I walked in revealed that my presence was about as welcome as cancer.

Proceeding according to the established script, I lapsed into type and in short order had words with a guy in the bar after he asked Mel out to dinner, then outside after the bar closed got into a brawl with another guy when he tried to give her his number. This time she didn't see the funny side. In fact she went ape-shit, calling me this that and the other, at the same time punching and scratching my face. I responded by jumping behind the wheel of her brand new Mercedes, starting the engine and trying to drive off. It was an automatic. I thought it was manual. By the time I realized I'd wrecked the gear box.

I awoke the next morning. They call it déjà vu. Another massive hangover and the memory of another night of mayhem. Now I knew for sure. Mel and I just weren't meant for one another.

I never spoke to or laid eyes on her again.

7

The best thing about working on *Friends*, or on any of the other sitcoms I would come to work on over the next few years, was the experience of being in front of a live audience. It was then you got a taste of the buzz which the cast of sitcoms enjoy on a regular basis. I recall the times working on *Friends* being shepherded to the set with the other extras along a narrow passageway underneath the stand (referred to in the States as bleachers) where the audience was sitting. There we were, like rats, sneaking along in the dark at the same moment as the cast was being introduced to the audience one by one and the entire soundstage shook with the thunderous roar of adulation let loose in response.

If, after this experience, I still harboured any illusions about my significance in the scheme of things, one episode of *Friends* in particular left me in no doubt. It came in a scene involving Matt Le Blanc (Joey) and David Schwimmer (Ross). It was a restaurant scene in which Ross is busy trying to woo a girl over dinner when suddenly Joey shows up and attempts to woo her away from him. I was cast as the only other customer in the place, directed to walk on twenty seconds after Matt Le Blanc enters the scene, take a seat at the bar and order a drink from the bartender, played by another extra.

Offstage, tucked in a tiny space awaiting my cue, there I was, with Matt Le Blanc standing pressed up against me waiting for the scene to begin. It was at that moment it occurred to me that he was on a million dollars an episode, while I was being paid fifty bucks a day. I couldn't even take comfort in the fact that he was a good five or six inches shorter than me. Even worse, at that moment Le Blanc decided to let one go. At least his shit stank the same.

Another popular show I worked on which provided a telling insight into the business was *ER*. As with *Friends*, I used to sit at home riveted to this show, impressed by the quality of the acting and the writing, not to mention the way they managed to replicate the bedlam and chaos of an Accident and Emergency unit in each episode. My first time on it I was booked to play a medical orderly. Our call time was a miserable 7am, which necessitated a 5.30am rise to be sure of getting there on time, especially as the casting director at Central had emphasized how stringent the show was about timekeeping and how if any of the extras were late they would be sent home with a black mark on their file, placing them in a bad light when it came to securing future work.

ER was another Warner Bros show, which meant going through the tortuous process of parking in a designated lot located across the other side of a busy main road from the soundstage, enduring an extensive security check at the pedestrian entrance to the studio (this was before 9/11. Post 9/11 the security checks were nothing short of forensic, involving a complete body search and an item by item search of all your possessions) followed by a long walk through a veritable full-sized town of soundstages, mock-up streets, shops and office blocks, all the while weighed down with your bags.

Bleary-eyed and stiff, I finally reached the relevant soundstage - Stage 3 or 4, I seem to recall - only for my stomach to hit the ground. Extras-holding was a cold, dark corner of an adjacent soundstage, where fifty or sixty people were crammed in so tight there was hardly room to stretch your arms. Even worse, craft service consisted of cheap instant coffee, bagels, doughnuts and bananas. With a typical day on *ER* being 10-12 hours in duration, it was always an arduous experience on this show. I think I worked on it a total of three times - as an orderly, a fireman, and a male nurse respectively. On the set they achieved that uniquely chaotic atmosphere using long steadicam shots and lots of background crosses. After I'd been in two or three scenes I completely lost interest, utterly miserable at knowing I was going to be spending the next ten hours cooped up in the corner of a cold, desolate soundstage seated next to a man in the final stages of whooping cough on one side and a lady who wouldn't or couldn't stop belching on the other. I ate so many doughnuts and bagels out of boredom I soon joined her.

An embarrassing incident took place while working on the Al Pacino movie *Simone*. I was booked to work on it as a guest at a movie awards after party. The movie is about a movie director, Pacino, who creates a virtual movie star called Simone. Suffice to say, it isn't among his best work. Anyway, all the extras had been fitted out in ball gowns and black dinner suits. It was a big scene and there must have been around three hundred extras. During a break between shots, I left extras holding and sat down on a crate about twenty feet away from where Pacino was sitting and watched him. It was one of those moments. There he was, just twenty feet away from me, Michael Corleone himself. I noticed him looking over his shoulder at me. Serpico was looking at me. I waved. Two minutes later I felt a tap on my shoulder. It was one of the production assistants. He had two guys from set security with him.

"Excuse me, sir," he said, "could I talk to you for a second?"

With the security guys walking behind me, I followed him all the way through the soundstage to the exit. The entire crew were watching, not to mention the extras. At the door the production assistant turned to me.

"I'm sorry, Mr Pacino doesn't want you on the set. He says you keep staring at him."

I looked at him.

"These gentlemen will be happy to escort you to wardrobe and from there to the parking lot and your car."

I was about to walk through the door, when I stopped. All of a sudden I was Tessio and we were in *The Godfather*.

"Tell Mike it was only business. I always liked him."

"Excuse me?" the production assistant said, bemusement

breaking out on his face.

"Tom...can you get me off the hook? For ol' times sake?"

"Sir, are you okay?"

I lowered my head and walked through the door. The guys from set security followed. Nobody fucks with Michael Corleone.

Even more embarrassing than this, however, was the time I was booked to play a dead guy. It was on some cop show I can't recall the name of now, but I do remember it was a big steadicam shot in which the principal actors, three of them, break down the door of an apartment with their guns drawn and rush through the place into the bathroom, where they find one of their fellow detectives – played by yours truly – lying dead, having been murdered.

As I took up position on the floor I decided it was time to get noticed. Rather than lie there with my eyes shut, I opted to open them wide, staring at the ceiling and contorting my features in a search for authenticity. I'm going to be the best dead guy these fuckers have ever seen, I thought to myself.

"Action!"

The door crashed open and the actors rushed in, screaming my character's name, the cameraman following behind with the steadicam, along with the sound guy holding the boom. Here they come and...*crash!* ...they enter the bathroom to find me lying on the floor.

"Cut!" the director screamed. "Who told that fuckin' extra to open his eyes?! Get him outta here!"

But, inevitably looking back, I soon began to rebel against the constant disrespect and ill-treatment an extra is expected to take as part and parcel of the job. On any given show or movie at least one or two members of the crew would bully, insult or humiliate some poor bastard or other, and in my time I witnessed many incidents of abuse. The ones that used to disgust me most were those involving pensioners, obviously down on their luck, being yelled at by some 20-year-old production assistant for not moving fast enough when instructed to do something; or by someone in the wardrobe department for having brought the wrong wardrobe. Craft service people, caterers, PAs, ADs, grips and more than a few principal actors saw nothing wrong with abusing people struggling to make ends meet on minimum wage.

There are two types who do extra work in Hollywood. The first are those who do it because they can't get anything better and need the pay, minimum wage or not. Falling into this category were the pensioners I just mentioned, people without a decent education, students working their way through college, and various others. The second type are those who want to make it in the business, aspiring actors who see it as a way of getting their SAG card and/or some on-set experience. Some, suffering from delusion, harbour the hope that they might get noticed on a set by a producer or director and be catapulted into a principle acting role. This is one of those persistent myths that bear no relation to reality. It never happens.

Starting out, I was stunned that people were so desperate to succeed they were willing to so readily place their pride and self-respect to one side. People who'd moved to Hollywood from other parts of the world chasing the dream were soon reduced to the existence of a worm at the hands of a caste system more rigid than any to be found on the Indian subcontinent.

Though starting out in the same vein, biting my tongue to the point where it was almost severed, it got to the point where began to talk back to the snooty wardrobe ladies, the abusive craft service people, the bullying PAs and ADs. I quickly gained a reputation for being a troublemaker and in time certain shows refused to book me.

However, the shit really hit the fan on the set of a low-budget martial arts movie one day.

The name of the movie was *Chickfighter*, which should tell you all you need to know when it comes to the quality of the project

- or lack thereof. It was a two day weekend gig and I'd only booked myself on it to get in some extra hours at the end of what had been a sparse week. The entire booking turned out to be an exercise in lies and duplicity from beginning to end. The casting director at Central Casting had instructed us to wear only upscale wardrobe (dress clothes), which had to be black or dark grey in colour, as we were booked to play diners at an expensive restaurant. The location was somewhere on Sunset Boulevard that we were given as an address only. I assumed it was some fancy restaurant or other that the production had taken over for the two days of the shoot.

I was wrong.

The location wasn't a fancy restaurant - no restaurant of any kind in fact. Instead it was an old disused warehouse. Worse, it turned out that we weren't there as upscale restaurant diners as we'd been told by the casting director who'd booked us, but spectators at an underground cage fighting competition. The casting director had lied in order to entice us into taking the booking in the first place and wearing dress clothes; the idea being that we look like high rollers betting on the fights.

All of the extras, around thirty of us, were miserable. Extras-holding turned out be nothing more than a makeshift tent on a patch of dirty ground adjacent to the set, and soon our shoes were covered in dirt and mud. The food was terrible and on set they were using a lot of smoke. Not only that, the scenes they were shooting contained a lot of profanity, which didn't bother me as much as it did some of the women who were present. The casting director should have forewarned us so that in cases where it was likely to cause offense people could have opted out. The entire booking was bogus and the set an unpleasant environment to be in from the very start. Regardless, I needed the money badly and on the first day, striking up a pleasant conversation with a group of my fellow sufferers, I was okay and felt confident I would be able stick it for the duration. A few decided not to return the following day, but I wasn't among them and was back bright and early intent on getting another full day of overtime under my belt.

At one point we were standing around waiting for the crew to set up the next shot, passing the time in hushed conversations. Suddenly this guy appeared, the producer, and started screaming at the top of his voice for us to shut up and be quiet, gesturing violently as the abuse flowed in our direction in one long stream of consciousness. Immediately I experienced that horrible sensation you get when you feel violated or threatened and get ready to mount a physical defence. In that moment I felt compelled say something.

I didn't just barge in right away, though. No, I waited instead for an opportune moment and enough time to have passed to allow tempers to cool. My opportunity came half an hour later back out in extras-holding, where I noticed the producer standing by himself smoking a cigarette. I made my approach.

'Excuse me, sir. I'm one of the extras and no disrespect intended, you were a little aggressive earlier. Some of the women are upset and ...'

'Who the fuck do you think you're talking to?' he screamed. 'Do you know who the fuck I am? When I say shush I mean shush!'

He was pointing his finger in my face. I tried to reply but he kept on yelling. Instinct took over. My right hand came up and punched him in the mouth. He staggered back a few steps, face transmitting shock. Seconds passed while he processed what had happened. Soon as he did he got right on the radio and started screaming that he was being attacked and needed assistance. Moments later the cast and crew came pouring out of the set like the 7th Cavalry. Within seconds they had me surrounded.

Bad enough being confronted by a mob, but when the producer began demanding that somebody call the cops I knew I was in trouble. I momentarily thought about taking off, but clearly this wasn't an option. They had my name, my address, and anyway by taking off I would be admitting guilt. No, I had no choice. I was going to have to stay and face the music. Fuck it.

As soon as the cops arrived, in the shape of three large LAPD officers sporting crew cuts and enough firepower to take down a herd of elephants, the producer began accusing me of attacking him without provocation. In this he was joined by members of the crew, none of whom had even witnessed the incident. The experience of watching it unfold was surreal, like being present as a spectator at your own execution.

In the end the cops, whom to be fair appeared sympathetic to my plight, had no alternative. Three witnesses had stepped forward to corroborate the producer's story that I'd assaulted him without provocation. The cops informed me that they were taking me in and booking me with assault. Just as I was being escorted over to their patrol car in handcuffs three girls, extras, who'd been part of the group I'd spent the weekend chatting to, appeared from nowhere and asked the officer in charge if they could have a word. Leaving me in the care of his colleagues, he walked off to the side with them. Whatever was being discussed was going to have a huge bearing on my fate.

Then they returned; the girls smiling at me as they passed on their way back to extras-holding, the officer in charge informing me that the girls had just informed him that the producer had in fact touched me first and therefore my action in punching him could now be considered self-defence.

'With this in mind,' the officer said in conclusion, 'do you now wish to press assault charges of your own?'

I looked at him, suddenly speechless.

'Yes, you do wish to press charges,' prompted one of the other two cops standing immediately to my right.

I nodded my assent and the officer in charge walked over to inform the producer, who throughout had been seated over to the side holding an icepack against his face while drinks and snacks were brought to him by various members of the crew. I couldn't hear the officer break the news, but I knew he had by the way the producer jumped up out of his chair to begin screaming and swearing at the top of his voice. The officer returned and told me to get my stuff and leave. He didn't need to tell me twice.

My car was parked in a lot fifteen minutes walk from the set. Just as I arrived one of the production's shuttle vans pulled up. Out hopped the girls who'd spoken up on my behalf. They'd been fired as soon as the cops left. I didn't know what to say, how to thank them for what they'd done, especially when they told me how they had tried to speak to the police officers the entire time I was being booked but were kept from doing so by members of the crew.

We hugged, exchanged numbers and went our separate ways. Pulling out of the parking lot onto Sunset Boulevard, I cranked up the stereo, rolled down the window and breathed in a lungful of that cool southern Californian night air.

8

Fortunately, Central Casting overlooked the incident and kept me on their books. This was down to the girls who had orginally come to my rescue calling them the next day to again speak up on my behalf. It also came to light that the casting agent who booked the extras had done so as a favour to the producer, whom she knew personally. It had not been an officially-sanctioned booking. This was an additional factor in my favour when it came to being exonerated by Central.

But this didn't alter the fact that producers and other crew members higher up the food chain looked upon extras as little better than cannon fodder, worthy of zero respect. Many times on set I'd talked to my fellow extras about the possibility of going on strike to improve our pay and conditions. Elaborating on the idea, I had posed the possibility of every extra in Hollywood going on strike for just one week and bringing the industry to a halt. Never more than one or two would agree or indicate any interest in this line of thinking. The vast majority would merely sit and listen for a few minutes, squirming uncomfortably in the hard plastic chair supplied grudgingly by the production, or in the canvas chairs they'd brought with them, before getting up and heading over to the craft service table; there to be molested for daring to pick up a piece of fruit or pour themselves a cup of coffee without going through the required ritual of supplication beforehand.

In truth I think they thought I was some kind of nut, a troublemaker to be avoided lest I interfere with their climb to wealth and fame. Oppressed, humiliated, maligned and bullied they may have been, but to them it was only a temporary state of affairs, the necessary 'paying of the dues' required of all who aspire to success in Hollywood. In this dystopia of desperation and delusion, the American Dream remained a living, breathing entity, one that belonged to all who were willing to abase themselves before it. Thus any attempt to instill a sense of class consciousness was doomed from the start.

The thing that every non-union extra wants from day one of his or her career, lusts after with the desire of a sixty-year-old on viagra for a playgirl, is a SAG card. It's all that matters and on every set, between two extras meeting for the first time, you can bet your last penny that one of the first questions to spill out of the mouth of one of them will be: 'Are you in the union?' If the answer to the question is in the affirmative, the questioner, if he or she is also in the union, will go on to discuss agents, casting directors, head shots - any of the myriad topics connected to getting ahead in the industry. If the questioner doesn't possess a SAG card they will study and scrutinize the lucky holder of one, trying to work out what he or she has that they do not, hoping if they stare long enough that whatever it is might somehow rub off on them. As for the recipient of this scrutiny, there is nothing more uncomfortable, and all you can do is extricate yourself from the situation as quickly and painlessly as possible whenever you encounter it.

The conventional way an extra could become eligible to join the union was to work under a SAG voucher on three separate occasions. These union vouchers were typically available for non-union extras in cases where a union extra failed to show up for a booking, leaving their voucher free to be handed to someone else. To be the lucky recipient of this voucher required the AD, or the person in charge of distributing the vouchers on set, to have already taken a liking to you beforehand (in most cases, given that the majority of ADs were males, you would find the grateful recipient of an AD's favour a young ingénue just arrived off the bus from Georgia or Michigan with nothing to recommend her other than a pair of long legs and/or a set of humungous mammary glands).

Casting directors were also able to allocate extra union

vouchers on occasion, which again normally required the forming of a personal relationship of some sort beforehand.

It was a system that lent itself to dishonesty and corruption, a microcosm of the entire industry it could be argued. The competitiveness and malice it produced was startling in its crudity when first encountered. But you soon learn that in Hollywood words such as propriety are not only laughed at but sneered at, lost in the stampede as people chase their dream. A few extras I spoke to revealed how they had bribed ADs to give them the vouchers they needed to be eligible to join the union. Others spoke of extras buying casting directors gifts, of girls taking male casting directors out to dinner and even, so the rumours went, providing sexual favours.

I got my own vouchers through a combination of luck, persistence and opportunism. The first I received from one of the casting directors at Central. Though we'd never met, and had only ever dealt with each other over the phone, booking me on one of her shows one day she casually informed me she was doing so on a union voucher. It was a stroke of good fortune which left me needing two more to finally be eligible to join that privileged fraternity of union extras with their nicer clothes, better and newer cars, and all-round aura of smug superiority.

Someone once said that in order to survive among wolves you have to be a wolf. The veracity of this wisdom was apparent in the change that took place in me after five months living and working in Hollywood. Darwin's theory of evolution comes down to the basic premise of survival of the fittest, the theory that only those species that are able to adapt to changes in their environment manage to survive in a process described as 'natural selection'. Plunged into the cauldron of fierce competition that is Hollywood, a town populated by men and women from all over the world who arrive consumed with the burning desire to grab the same limited opportunities, I had to adapt pronto if I did not want to end up on a flight home within a few short months, sharing the fate of those who find soon after arriving that they don't have what it takes. This is no surprise when you consider that the monumental effort involved in surviving on the minimum wage of a non-union extra or a security guard in Los Angeles means that just one mistake, one slip, and you're fucked.

I'd come with a few thousand in savings. But having to buy a car, an old Chevy Caprice that fortunately proved reliable even if thirsty, as well as pay the deposit on an apartment, furnish it and meet the rent every month thereafter, in no time I began edging perilously close to the edge of financial disaster. Not for me the luxury of rich parents, or even comfortably-off parents, to whom I could turn when the going got tough. Not for me either the safety net of savings or investments. No, I was on my own, dangerously and precipitously perched on a financial tightrope, and with each passing day the pressure grew.

Down to my last nine hundred bucks, and only pulling in a couple a hundred a week, I realized I would have to take some drastic action. The solution lay in getting my hands on a SAG card and ensuring that I got booked to work every day at the higher rate of a union extra. The lucky few I'd met who were in this position made a good living and I had to force myself among them. But how, that was the question. What could I possibly do to make it happen?

The answer came to me whilst working on a TV show as a detective. In a scene with the principal actor, I got close enough to place him under scrutiny. What did he have that I didn't? Was it something he'd been endowed with by Mother Nature that I had not? Did he possess better genes? What was it?

The answer turned out to be more prosaic than you might think. What he possessed that I did not was a decent suit. He was dressed in an expensive, designer suit, exquisitely cut and tailored, while I and my fellow extras were not. The contrast was inescapable. While we looked like refugees from a charity shop, he looked like... well, the principle actor on a TV show. Simply put, if I was going to stand any chance in this town I would have to invest in a good suit. I did exactly that with the last of my savings and the change in fortunes occurred almost overnight. Resplendent now in a charcoal-grey single-breasted designer number, suddenly ADs began calling Central Casting and booking me on their shows by name. Within weeks I'd received six or seven union vouchers, never mind the two I required to be eligible to join. The only problem now was getting my hands on the 1500 dollar fee required up front for the privilege. That's right: just to be allowed into SAG you had to shell out a large chunk of change, the kind of money I not only did not have but wasn't remotely close to having.

The opportunity to make this kind of money came completely out of the blue one day. I was at the gym when this older guy approached me. He was one of the regular small-time fight promoters who were always hanging around, mostly full of shit. Whenever I came across him we'd pass pleasantries, but never anything more than that. This is why I was so taken aback when he said: 'Hey, J, are you looking for work right now?'

I hesitated before nodding in the affirmative.

'I have a buddy who needs help with some asshole who's giving his girl a hard time. Pays two grand. You interested?'

Again, I nodded, though without really thinking about what I might be getting into, more concerned about the bills that were piling up fast and the fact I was hardly making enough to make ends meet. Accordingly, two grand was a fortune to me.

'Okay, gimme your number and I'll have him call ya,' he said. 'He'll refer to it as the paint-job over the phone, just so you know.'

The call came in around seven that evening. 'Yo…this J?'

'Yes.'

'Hey, how are ya buddy? This is Burt. I believe you spoke to a friend of mine earlier about a paint job.'

'Ah-huh.'

'He says you might be interested.'

'Ah-huh.'

'Says you'll do it for two grand.'

'Well ...'

'Great. Let's meet. How about Wednesday night? I'll let ya know then exactly what I need.'

He went on to give me directions to a hamburger place somewhere out in the middle of Agoura Hills in canyon country, about an hour's drive from Hollywood up the 405 North without traffic. With traffic you were talking anything from an hour and a half to two hours for the same journey. It ended up taking me two.

Driving up there really gave me a sense of my place in the scheme of things. The wide expanse of dry scrub and cacti stretched out on either side of the freeway was offset by high mountains in the distance. I drank it all in, thinking how hard life must have been for the pioneers who arrived a couple of centuries before with their belongings in rickety wagons. Then I considered the indigenous people who'd been displaced and ethnically cleansed as those first pioneers were followed by wave after wave of settlers from the East. Sitting in traffic, it struck me how paradise was turned into a living hell for those whose only crime was to live on land coveted by others.

I finally reached the Agoura Hills exit and arrived at the outdoor mini mall where I'd been requested to meet my contact. Like the other plethora of mini malls that cover LA County north to south and east to west, it contained the usual tired complement of fast food and retail outlets. I walked into the hamburger place as instructed. Immediately I picked out the guy from the gym and his buddy whom I'd spoken to briefly over the phone. They were seated at opposite ends of a long counter, obviously with the intention of appearing alone and unknown to one other. It hadn't worked.

'Hey, J,' the one from the gym said as he rose from his seat at the counter. He was sweating and his eyes darted right and left. I nodded whereupon he looked round and gestured to the other guy at the far end. He turned back to me. 'Let's talk outside.'

I followed him out to the parking lot. Behind us seconds later came his friend. He introduced himself as Burt while vigorously shaking me by the hand. The gold Rolex on his wrist bounced up and down in the process.

'So, did Hank explain what it is we're looking for?' he said.

I nodded.

'I just want the prick slapped around a bit. Nothing too crazy.'

He went on to explain that he wanted this done because the guy in question was giving him a hard time over the fact he was dating his ex. When he gave me a card with his officer number on it and it turned out to be the number of a sauna and massage parlour, it all started to make sense. This guy Burt was a pimp.

Hank took off at this point. His role had been to provide initial introduction and he was keen to leave us to it. As soon as he was gone Burt drove me up to the location in his Ferrari. We soon arrived in a suburban neighbourhood of bland apartment blocks, occupied by the kind of people who believed wholeheartedly in God while hating blacks, Arabs, Mexicans, gays, and others who in their eyes don't measure up. It was the land of the small and narrow-minded, of people so brainwashed by the myth of America and the American Dream they no longer know their arse from their elbow. Perennially fucked by a system they viewed as sacrosanct, theirs were lives of dull monotony and blind consumerism. I'd only been in Agoura Hills for half an hour and already I was depressed.

Burt showed me where the guy parked his truck, a red pickup, and the path he would take from the parking lot to the entrance to his apartment building. The path was unlit, quiet and bordered on either side by tall bushes. It was the perfect spot for an ambush. He then drove back out of the estate, up the road a little and turned into another estate on the opposite side. He suggested this as the best place to leave the car while undertaking the business at hand. Satisfied that I'd been fully briefed we returned to the mini mall. Once the deed was done I was to meet him back here and he would square me up.

It was coming up eight o'clock. According to Burt the guy arrived home from work sometime between 8.15 and 8.30. It was time to set off. He walked me over to my car in an excited state, delighted I could tell that the object of his grudge was about to be dealt with. When we reached my car he laughed.

'Shit, J, is this what you're drivin'? Man, we gotta get you some decent wheels. This thing looks about ready to fall apart.'

I looked at him before opening the door and getting in. He told me good luck as I turned the key in the ignition. I nodded, put it in reverse, pulled out of the space and drove off, leaving him behind in my rearview.

I reached the prearranged spot, parked and turned off the engine. I was surrounded by darkness and silence. The streets were completely deserted. Inside the houses people were feasting on their regular diet of sitcoms, reality TV, and celebrity gossip. I waited fifteen minutes, got out of the car and walked over to the brick wall adjacent. The only noise was provided by crickets chirruping in chorus and the occasional sound of a vehicle coming along the road in either direction. I clenched my fists tight and began punching the wall as hard as I could. I punched it five or six times with each hand until the skin broke and blood appeared on both knuckles. Then I got back into the car and took a slow drive back to the mini mall.

Burt was waiting in his car. He saw me coming and got out. I parked, also got out, and walked over to him. His face was red and glistening with sweat.

'So how'd it go?' he said, anticipation wrapped round every word like a python round its prey. I held out both hands with the palms facing down, showing him the blood and the scrapes on my knuckles.

'Yeah? You get 'im good?'

I nodded. He reached into his pocket and brought out a wad of cash.

'Fuckin' great. Two grand we said, right?'

I nodded.

'Tell ya what, fuck it, let's make it twenty-five hundred. Sounds like you did a good job.'

He counted out the money and handed it over.

'I'll call you in a coupla days to make sure everything's all right.' Then he shook my hand. 'You're a good guy, J. Just be careful drivin' that tin can.' He said this chuckling while nodding in the direction of the Chevy. 'I just hope you make it back to Hollywood in one piece.'

I got back in the car and drove off, turning out of the mini mall and joining the freeway heading south in the direction of Hollywood.

A few days later Burt left a message on my voicemail, something to the effect that he'd just seen the 'wall' and it didn't look like it had any paint on it. I had his work number and called back early the next morning, knowing he wouldn't be there and the call would go straight to his voicemail. I left a message professing shock at the possibility I'd made a mistake and painted the wrong wall, making sure to volunteer my services should he want the 'paint job' redone.

I never heard from him again.

The important thing was I now had the money to join SAG.

As it turned out, my timing in joining the union could not have been worse. The annual hiatus had just begun, when the movie and television industry shuts down for three months during the summer, and there was no way I could afford to go three months without work. Thankfully though salvation arrived - this time in the shape of Gabriel.

Originally from Sweden, Gabriel had lived in Japan for a

couple of years, where he trained and competed as a professional kickboxer. He decided to move to Hollywood with the intention of finding work in martial arts movies. Unfortunately for him, by the time he arrived Hollywood had stopped making martial arts movies. We met one day on the set of some shitty TV show. Like me he was working as an extra. Unlike me he didn't last very long and quit. He was six feet six inches tall, weighed in at around 250 lbs, and made Dolph Lungdren look like a baby by comparison. Both hailing from Europe, living a similar hand to mouth existence far from home, we became fast friends.

Due to his considerable size and presence, Gabriel found himself in demand to work as a doorman and bodyguard in Hollywood. He worked for a company that provided security teams to work celebrity parties, high-end private functions, movie premieres, and various other events. He had a lot of clout with the company and was able to get me a start. Even though I'd vowed never to work in security again after my bad experience at the Mondrian Hotel, those lofty principles were superseded by the more important one of keeping a roof over my head. What Gabriel failed to tell me was that the company also provided security for various bars and nightclubs, which is the level at which new recruits began until they'd proven themselves and were chosen to be part of the so-called elite group that worked the better jobs. Consequently, the first place they sent me to work was about as far from a movie premiere or star-studded celebrity party as it was possible to get. It was called *Sombreros*, a Mexican-themed bar and nightclub located on the Universal Citywalk in North Hollywood.

The Citywalk is a large shopping arcade located adjacent to Universal Studios, complete with movie theaters, restaurants, bars, souvenir shops, and various tourist attractions. Imagine a neon wilderness which uses up more electricity than the whole of sub-Saharan Africa on a nightly basis, catering to people who liked to gorge themselves on hamburgers, hotdogs, and milkshakes, every one obese and proud. To watch them was to leave you in no doubt that humanity was doomed.

Sombreros was located at the very end of the mall on the second level.

Dressed in suit and tie, I approached the guy standing on the other side of the rope at the entrance and as instructed asked for Benny. He directed me over to a group of guys who were standing huddled round a fat guy addressing them in a booming voice. This was Benny, head of security, and I joined the back of the group and listened in.

'So I don't want any of you guys standing around with your hands in your pockets like you're hangin' out. We gotta be professional at all times. Make sure your flashlights are working, make sure your cuffs are on your belt where you can reach em. And, remember, be vigilant.

'Any questions?'

There were no questions.

'Okay. Let's go to work.'

At this everyone dispersed. During the briefing I'd counted twelve guys, which struck me as a lot for one place. *For what reason,* I mused. *Don't tell me I've been sent to work in a war zone.*

Benny was distributing radios when I approached. He was short and fat. He wore his hair cropped to the bone and his face looked like it had taken its fair share of punches. Like most of the guys, he had on an ill-fitting suit. Unlike the others he also had on a pair of leather gloves and on his feet instead of dress shoes a pair of black work boots.

I introduced myself.

'You're late,' he told me. 'This is your first and final warning. I run a tight ship here and I got no time for flakes, time-wasters or assholes. You understand me?'

I said nothing.

'Okay, I'm gonna pair you up with Brian. He'll show ya the ropes. Watch what he does and do the same. You bring cuffs an' a flashlight?'

'No.'

'Next time you show up without cuffs an a flashlight, I'll send your ass home. I ain't got time to fuck around. Shape up an' get your shit together.'

He got on the radio and called Brian. A minute or so later a big guy with red hair and a ruddy complexion came swaggering through the door from inside the place. Benny introduced us, we shook hands, and off we went into the club.

It was a big place all right, comprising two levels, with a large bar and dance floor downstairs and upstairs the same, only slightly smaller. I noticed a lot of staff running around, which could only mean they were expecting a large crowd. I asked Brian about this and he assured me it would be crazy by midnight, with both levels packed out.

I was impressed at how seriously these guys were taking their job, especially considering how little we were being paid. Throughout, Brian was in radio contact with the other guys and they all looked and carried themselves professionally. In all my time never had I seen the job approached as seriously and with as much enthusiasm.

Despite taking the role so seriously, Brian was relaxed, affable and easy to get along with at the same time. To look at him he appeared your stereotypical redneck. In fact, with his bright red hair and pale skin he looked more Scottish than I did.

Sure enough, as he'd assured me, come midnight the place was jumping, the atmosphere ramped up by loud Mexican music, which verily assaulted the senses. A young crowd, they were going crazy on the dancefloor. The guys all seemed to carry themselves with attitude, while the girls were mostly feminine and conscious of their appearance.

I spent the entire night traipsing around the place at Brian's side like an idiot, moving between floors, helping keep a wary eye on proceedings. Each of the guys occupied a certain spot throughout the place and never moved an inch unless they had good reason to. Brian explained that before the company took over the security contract there were fights every night and stabbings on a regular basis. But since they moved in three months ago there'd been hardly any trouble at all apart from the odd incident.

Benny was stationed at the front door dealing with the crowd outside waiting to come in and I didn't see him again until the night ended and we cleared everybody out. As soon as this was done he called us all downstairs for a debriefing to go over the night's proceedings.

It was at this point that I realized I was among morons. Where before I'd been impressed by the professionalism and diligence of the security operation in the place, I now viewed it as a joke consisting of a bunch of grown men pretending to be cops.

As Benny dissected the night in minute detail, I stood at the back and took the opportunity to study my fellow security guards up close. They were all shapes and sizes, with only two or three who looked to be in any kind of physical shape. They were not an impressive bunch to look at, which only made their attitude and approach to the job all the more silly.

'...an' I wanna acknowledge the contribution of J, the new guy on the team.'

All eyes turned to me as Benny continued. 'His attitude was excellent; he was sharp, focused and disciplined. He's proved himself a valuable addition and I'd like you all to join me in welcoming him aboard.'

This was followed by a round of applause.

Never have I felt a greater urge to depart a place or situation as I did then.

9

Fortunately, I only had to endure a month at *Sombreros* before the security company moved me elsewhere.

As mentioned, in addition to providing security for various bars and nightclubs, the company also handled the security for various celebrity and Hollywood parties, movie premieres, and other high profile one-off events. It was considered a privilege to be chosen to work at these events, marking you out as a member of the company's elite crew. When I arrived for my first job as part of this 'elite crew' the difference between the guys I'd worked with over at *Sombreros* and these guys was immediately obvious. Every one of them looked impressive - tall, well built and capable - and they carried themselves accordingly. Out of them all Gabriel easily stood out most. The owners of the company, Dennis and Hal, viewed him as their posterboy, and they never lost an opportunity to parade him in front of the clients Tonight's assignment was a private party being thrown by the rap artist and producer variously known as Puff Daddy, Sean Combes, and P Diddy at a Bel Air mansion to celebrate the MTV Awards, which that year were being held in LA. The guest list comprised a who's who of celebrities from the worlds of music, film and sports.

We'd been instructed to meet up in a quiet side street on the edge of Beverly Hills, where Hal broke out the radios and gave us a rundown of what to expect when we arrived at the venue. There were ten of us, which struck me as a small squad of guys to work such a high-profile event. It made sense, however, when Hal informed us that five different security firms had been hired to work the party. In recognition of our quality, he continued, we were assigned the all-important task of manning the front entrance.

What he said did not strike me as bullshit at the time, though clearly it was, and if the desired effect was to get us psyched up and motivated it certainly worked, at least judging by the chests that were puffed out a little more and jaws clenched tighter in response.

Up to the location we headed in a convoy of beat-up, secondhand cars and trucks, following Hal in his split-new, freshly polished black Suburban four-wheel drive with tinted windows. Hal had worked as a doorman in bars and clubs in Hollywood for many years and was a well-known face, not to mention a well-respected one. Dennis's background in security comprised a career in the US Secret Service and working on personal security assignments for a variety of high-end clients. Neither of them were much to look at, but each possessed that brand of confidence which only comes with experience. In LA they were both known as men who could get the job done. Dennis had a firearms permit and carried a gun, as did a couple of the other guys, and I resolved to be anywhere but there if and when the bullets started flying.

We arrived at the location - not so much a mansion as a massive residential compound set in acres of land - and pulled up on a piece of wasteground set aside at the back of the house as the designated parking lot for those working the event - in other words, the help. In terms of size and sheer decadent splendor it was a place the like of which I had only ever seen in pictures or read about in magazines.

Once parked, we entered the compound via a gate at the rear and from there proceeded to walk to the front of the house through a long underground passage where on either side, locked behind a steel grill, were stacked thousands of bottles of wine. The passage put me in mind of a medieval castle; and when we at last emerged on the other side we found ourselves in a large courtyard surrounded on three sides by top of the range, luxury cars. A massive fountain, baroque in style, stood pride of place in the middle of the courtyard, and it was obvious that the owner - the original owner who'd had the place built, that is - had attempted to achieve a French chateau-type elegance in both layout and design. In this he'd failed. Vulgarity not elegance was the word that sprang to mind.

Indeed, the size, luxury and ostentation was way over the top, and I couldn't help thinking how outrageous it is that one human being can live in such comfort and luxury while just a few miles away on the other side of the city, in downtown LA, thousands were bedding down for night in doorways and back alleys surrounded by filth and rats.

Hal led us in the direction of the front gate amid the hustle and bustle that was unfolding everywhere you looked. Three massive marquee tents had been set up in the grounds and scores of waiters, catering staff, bar tenders, managers, and security guards were rushing back and forth, busy preparing for the arrival of the guests. The event promoters, three of them, were standing in a huddle at the gate engrossed in conversation. Hal instructed us to wait while he went over to speak to them, taking Gabriel with him for effect.

While the rest of us waited my eyes feasted on the amount of food that had been set up on long tables adjacent. It was a spread to rival any you would have found at the court of Louis XIV.

'Wow, look at the size of that mothafuckin' spread,' one of the guys announced, as if reading my thoughts.

'Maybe we'll get a sample later,' another commented.

'Don't hold your breath, man. They got dogs and cats to feed first.'

'Should be some fine lookin' bitches coming through this place tonight.'

'Yeah and none of 'em interested in eatin' out at Burger King either.'

'Fuck you.'

'You'll have a better chance of fucking me than any of the hotties at this party tonight, motherfucker.'

Hal and Gabriel returned a few minutes later and we gathered round to receive our instructions. Along with four others, I was assigned to work the shit-detail. This involved being stationed at the bottom of the long winding hill that led up to the main gate in order to provide back up to the two girls who were going to be doing the guest list down there. The idea behind doing it this way - checking off the names of arriving guests while they were still in their vehicles instead of allowing them to drive all the way to the top of the hill, park, and then arrive at the front gate before being checked off the list - was to prevent what they liked to call in the business out here a 'cluster fuck' of people at the main gate. It was one of those ideas that sounded good in theory but which in practice soon proved a disaster.

In no time a long line of vehicles had formed in the street at the bottom of the hill as people descended on the party en masse. They soon became agitated at the length of the time they were being forced to wait while the girls checked the names of the occupants in each vehicle against the names on the guest list. The resulting frustration was articulated in a crescendo of car horns and some of them screaming out their windows for us to 'hurry the fuck up!'

A high proportion of those on the guest list had brought people with them who weren't. When we pointed this out many became hostile and abusive, demanding to talk to the promoter, demanding that their guest or guests be allowed in with statements like 'do you know who the fuck I am? You're just a two-bit security guard and you're telling me I can't get in?'

This was bad enough. But when people began getting out of their vehicles to make their way up to the house on foot, bad gave way to disastrous. In fact things got so bad we had to put the call out for reinforcements. Gabriel and four of the other guys came running down the hill moments later. Unfortunately, their arrival proved a case of too little too late. Despite forming ourselves into a thin line at the bottom of the hill, the crowd managed to break through and we found ourselves in the ignominious position of following them up the hill to the front gate, defeated and bedraggled.

A couple of the guys took it personally and got themselves all bent out of shape and ready to fight. As for me, I thought it hilarious, the sight of so many people so desperate to get in to a party they were willing to trade their dignity in the process.

At the front gates the crowd swelled, pushing and shoving against the crash barriers that had been erected. All the guys were now standing behind the barriers in a last line of defence. Mike made futile attempts to get the crowd to disperse with announcements through a megaphone to the effect that only those on the guest list would be allowed in. Nobody budged an inch. Instead they stayed put and shouted him down.

Next, one of the promoters tried to get the crowd to disperse, though again without success. Finally, the man in charge of the house arrived on the scene and announced that the party was closed, that they were at capacity and no one, whether their name was on the guest list or not, would now be getting in and to please disperse.

It didn't work. In fact, worse, the crowd responded by pushing forward in a last ditch determined effort to break through the barriers. If the cops hadn't arrived when they did people would have been hurt. As it was, I ended up with a sore face as a result of a wild punch thrown by somebody in the crowd as it surged forward.

The cops didn't mess around and immediately declared the party closed, instructing the organizers to turn the music off and the guests to vacate the property. It seems there'd been a deluge of complaints from residents living in the street about the noise and general mayhem. These residents were very rich and therefore very influential people and the cops had shown up in force and were taking no nonsense.

Gradually, in small groups out they came, a who's who of A-list movie actors, celebrities and sports stars. The manner and extent to which people fawned over them, the way the valets ran like maniacs to get them their limos, Rolls Royces, Mercs, and top-of-the-range cars of every description was nauseating - a scene straight out of Caligula's Rome, it struck me while watching it unfold. I noticed how even the cops were deferential to them, thinking to myself that if this was a party in, say, South Central or East LA, frequented by poor blacks and Latinos, it would be a completely different story. In that situation you could guarantee the cops would adopt a far more heavy-handed approach, ready to use force at the drop of a hat.

Later that night I drove home with mixed feelings. Is this really an industry and a culture I want to be part of? Is this my objective in life? To join the ranks of an elite few who live in decadent luxury while the majority scrape and struggle to make ends meet?

I parked my beat-up Chevy in the parking garage and walked on through the alley leading out to Sycamore Avenue. It was a typical night in Hollywood, complete with the ubiquitous police chopper hovering overhead, drug dealers standing on the corner, people spilling out of bars and clubs, and a pungent smell of decay exacerbated by the summer heat.

Outside the entrance to the apartment building a small group of guys were sat on the steps drinking and smoking. I made my way between them to the door, opened it and entered. Over the stain-covered carpet I walked to my apartment. By the time I walked in, switched on the light and surveyed my living quarters, I was depressed. A secondhand mattress on the floor was my bed. It was augmented by a secondhand writing table and chair, a secondhand armchair, a TV that didn't get proper reception, a small CD player, and a laundry basket in the corner. I had one room, a tiny kitchen area, shower and toilet. The beige carpet on the floor was way past its best and no matter how hard and often I cleaned the place, a musty smell refused to budge.

I undressed, had a quick shower, read for half an hour and then switched off the light. I drifted off to sleep wondering if I'd be able to stay the course. I didn't think so.

When we weren't working, Gabriel and I would go out drinking. In Hollywood being seen in the right places with the right people is all-important, and on any given night there are club promotions going on all over town, each vying for that all-important A-list crowd. The promoters of these nights are celebrities in their own right, known by everyone who is anyone on the party circuit. In my time Jennifer was considered number one, her clubs the most popular and hardest to get into. She had the personality of your average pirana fish. If she didn't like you, didn't think you were important enough to be allowed access into one of her clubs, she would let you know in the most insulting way imaginable. In contrast, Howard was charming and always respectful. You still might not get in to one of his clubs, but at least you'd be rejected with a smile. Those two were the main promoters in Hollywood, the top dogs as it were, but snapping at their heels were others, all hoping to catch some of whatever Jennifer and Howard had and be propelled to the status of party and club promoter to the stars.

On any Monday, Wednesday or Thursday, the big party nights in LA, you'd find the likes of Leonardo DiCaprio, Britney Spears, Mark Wahlberg, and every other young actor you care to name at the time downing champagne cocktails surrounded by an entourage of trust-fund brats, aspiring actresses, and other assorted hangers-on. It was quite something to see close up. Half the LA Lakers basketball team might also be in attendance, again surrounded by various hangers-on. Certain nights, in particular at that time Wednesday nights at Las Palmas, a hip-hop crowd saw such luminaries from the world of black music and entertainment as Snoop Doggy Dogg, Dr Dre, Janet Jackson, and Jamie Foxx whooping it up.

Hugh Hefner and the four or five young blondes who accompanied him everywhere was a regular on the party circuit. He'd pull up to the entrance to wherever he was headed in the back of a stretch limo and jump out with his clutch of Playmates behind him. Whenever I saw him I couldn't make my mind up whether to laugh or cry. He always appeared to me like a man who slept tied to a radiator to ward off rigor mortis. From what I heard, his own parties at the Playboy Mansion were notorious affairs, redolent of ancient Rome at the zenith of its vast empire. To see him out and about, a man in his late seventies at the time, in the company of girls young enough to be his great granddaughters, was to see nature corrupted. Only in the rarefied environment of Hollywood would he even be possible.

Speaking of Las Palmas, I worked there for a few weeks and it easily proved the most stressful security job I had in all my time in Hollywood. For every celebrity in the place on a Wednesday night there were ten gang members, hustlers, and/or thugs. The last thing any of these guys would countenance was a white boy with a strange accent telling them what to do and when to do it. I would arrive for work, having sunk a couple of whiskies beforehand, plant myself in a corner and try to remain as inconspicuous as possible. The place was always packed to over capacity and it was all you could do to keep your sanity. There may have been a law against smoking in public spaces in California, but here it did not apply. On the contrary, in this place on a Wednesday night people smoked wherever and whatever they liked.

I got fired after six weeks or so after getting embroiled in a physical altercation with the head doorman. His name was Sam, and though nice and perfectly friendly to me when I first started working there, within a couple of weeks he was having a go. He particularly liked mimicking my Scottish accent in front of the staff and a few of the regular customers. This he did while high on the cocaine he snorted at regular intervals on any given night.

He was best friends with the manager, a wannabe actor named Bob, and the two of them would spend their time trying to get girls up to the office. Whenever they succeeded, they would re-emerge afterwards and go round the guys bragging about their exploits. Not satisfied with that they would also invite us to sniff their fingers. Yes, they were a couple of sleazy bastards.

On this particular night, the place closed, we'd just succeeded in the always stressful task of clearing everyone out. I was standing by the door talking to a girl who was a regular at the club whom I'd got to know and become friendly with. Sam meanwhile was standing in a group at the bar enjoying an after hours drink when he looked over and called out:

'Hey, J, why don't you show her the car you're drivin'. That should do it.'

Everybody laughed. Moments later the girl left and I wandered through to the back office to punch out and grab my jacket. By the time I re-emerged, Sam had forgotten all about me and was engrossed in conversation with his friends at the bar.

I left the club to begin my regular ten-minute walk along Hollywood Boulevard to Sycamore Avenue and home. Cars were still pulling out of the parking lot on the other side of the street. There were Humvees, BMWs, Mercs, Porsches, and Lexuses. It was a cool night. The usual complement of homeless were hunkered down in shop doorways, covered in old blankets and coats. I reached the corner of Hollywood Boulevard and stopped. It was no use. I couldn't let it go. I turned and headed back in the direction of the club.

When I walked back in Sam, Bob and the others were still standing drinking and laughing by the bar. Sam had his back to me as I approached. Tapping him on the shoulder, I asked him if I could have a quick word.

'Sure.'

I led him over to the side.

'What's up?' he said.

My right hand formed itself into a fist, came up and smacked him in the mouth. He reeled over, turning away at the same time. I gave him a toe-poke up the arse to send him on his way.

A few of the girls started screaming, while Bob and other members of staff came rushing over to help Sam, who was on the floor holding his face. I turned, marched to the door, threw it open and walked back out into the night. I walked along a deserted and desolate Hollywood Boulevard over the world-famous Walk of Fame. A full moon was suspended in a clear sky and here I was again - out of a job with the rent due at the end of the month.

Experientia docet stultos.

Experience teaches fools.

10

That success in the movie industry comes down to who you know is a well-known truism. And, yes, while it may be a truism applicable to business in general, when it comes to Hollywood it is one written in stone.

In my own case, I'd been writing screenplays in Scotland for five years with zero success before deciding to uproot and move over here. I had arrived believing that dedication and perseverance was all a person required in order to fulfil their ambitions in life. I couldn't have been more wrong.

Even to get a movie script read and considered in Hollywood is a monumental task; everyone, and I mean everyone in LA, is writing a screenplay, with a staggering 80,000 new screenplays registered with the Writers Guild of America every year. And while no official figure is available for the number of screenplays that aren't registered, you can bet it's a good few thousand more. Of course the vast majority of those are garbage. Even so, eighty thousand is a shitload of competition in a business that churns out a tiny fraction of that number of movies in a year. A lot of money is also invested in the development side of the industry, paying for scripts that are destined to end up sitting on a shelf gathering dust. But even here the odds of having a project picked up are massive. This is why the big studios only deal with a relatively small group of trusted agents and managers when it comes to reading and considering new material. In fact, even independent producers will only read material that comes to them via a trusted source.

What this means is that for new people like me, arriving fresh off the boat with zero connections, just getting an agent, any agent, is akin to climbing a mountain in a pair of roller skates. After a year of hundreds of query letters to agents and producers all over town, I found myself no further forward in this regard than I'd been when I first arrived. I grew despondent, gradually lost enthusiasm and, worse, belief that I would ever break through.

The plan had been to spend two or three years at most establishing a career before moving back to the UK to continue working from there. However, after just one year in LA in which I'd met countless writers, directors and actors who'd been here much longer than me and were still struggling, I learned that the average amount of time it took before those who were established had managed to break through was between 10 and 15 years. Story after story of struggle and disappointment, of near misses and hopes dashed, I heard and digested. One guy I worked beside at the Mondrian Hotel, named Luke, had been in LA fifteen years trying to establish himself as a full-time actor. He'd moved here from Ohio and had worked as a bellboy in hotels non stop since. At 46 years of age this could hardly be considered progress, yet there he was, still plugging away, spending his well-earned cash on acting lessons, headshots and all the other scams designed to exploit the desperation of those struggling to make it.

Another bellboy at the Mondrian had studied at Julliard in New York, one of the most prestigious drama schools around, taking out thousands of dollars in loans to sustain himself in the process. Yet after five years in LA all he had to show for his expensive education was a paltry three lines in a daytime soap.

Based on the aforementioned examples, my breakthrough, when it came, arrived completely out of the blue.

Angela was someone I knew from my previous stint in LA. She owned a vintage boutique in West Hollywood and called me up one day and asked if I would like to help out at a warehouse sale of old stock she was organizing. She needed someone to help load the truck and drive it to the venue where the sale was taking place. There I would help unload, set up, and then reverse the process two days later when the sale ended. It paid a hundred bucks a day, and since I was in no position to turn down work of any kind, I was happy to accept the offer.

Angela had a couple of girls working for her. During the course of the two days I worked helping her set up the sale, I got talking to them. One of them, Zara, hailed from Brooklyn, and her vocabulary was littered with expletives to prove it. During the course of one exchange, she told me she'd recently begun dating a guy who managed writers and directors and was looking for new talent. Like her, she elaborated, he hailed from New York.

Hearing this and sensing an opening, I told her I was a writer. More than that, I told her that I'd won awards for writing back in the UK (a complete lie), and that if she passed my details on to her new boyfriend and anything came of it - i.e. if money changed hands as a result - I would cut her in for a small commission. She took my contact details, assuring me she would pass them on, and that was that. I didn't really expect anything to come from it, if I'm being honest, especially as Zara had already made it clear that she hated everything about the movie industry and wanted no part of it. However, in my position I had to take advantage of every opportunity or opening whenever they came along, regardless of how slim or unlikely.

Just over a week later I received a message on my voicemail: 'Hey, J, this is Tom Mickelson over at Pilot Films. I got your details from Zara. She tells me you're a writer from Scatland. Do me a favour and give me a call when you get this. Zara probably told you I represent writers. Lemme know what you got and maybe we can work something out.'

I called him back the very next morning, gave him a quick rundown of the scripts I'd written, and from those he asked to see three. The same afternoon they were on their way to his office in a brown envelope. A couple of weeks later I was sat in his office with him and Jack, his partner and owner of the company, discussing the one script of mine they liked and wanted to develop into a movie.

During this initial meeting both of them were effusive about the possibilities of the script attracting interest within the industry. In the meantime they would take me on as a client and send me out on meetings with various producers around town to try and get me work on other projects as a writer for hire.

It's amazing what hope does for a person. Previously, I had been trudging from set to set and studio lot to studio lot, growing ever more despairing. The initial excitement of working and walking around Paramount, Sony, Warner Bros, and Disney studios had more than worn off. To many people around the world these were legendary places, filled with history and magic, but after a while I couldn't have cared less. Outside each of the many sound stages on the Warner Bros lot, for example, plaques on the wall were inscribed with the names of all the big movies that had been shot there going back decades. When I first started working at these places, I would often stop to read them and be impressed to learn that I was standing outside the soundstage where great movies like *Gone with the Wind, The Godfather,* and *The Sting* had been made years before. I remember vividly working at Warner Bros one day on a terrible TV show the name of which escapes me now. We were shooting outside in a part of the lot known as Midwestern Town. We'd been there since six in the morning, around a hundred of us, walking back and forth in a large street scene on a particularly hot day. Making things worse was the fact it was a production where the extras had to pay for their own lunch in the commissary. As poor as I was I made do with bagels, doughnuts and coffee from the craft service trolley. Extras-holding was in a mock-up café around the corner from where the action was taking place. I was sat there in my chair, contemplating my fate, when one of the regular Warner Bros walking tours came by. The guide was in the process of naming the various classic movies that were shot in this very location back in days of yore. He stopped outside the café where I was sat among some of my fellow extras and proceeded to announce that it was here, in this very spot, where the Paris cafe scenes in *Casablanca* with Humphrey Bogart and Lauren Bacall were shot.

But like I said, the novelty of all that wears off after a while when you're struggling to get by. The stories you hear about people being plucked from obscurity in Hollywood is a myth, responsible it has to be said for attracting mugs like me to the place from over the world, people who end up working the shitty, menial jobs as bartenders, security guards, valets, waitresses, and the worst of the lot - movie and television extras.

As for the tiny few who suddenly seem to burst onto the scene overnight as the next big thing, you can bet they worked their way to that point over years of acting classes, auditions, and rejection. For successful writers, directors and producers it's no different; they've all invested years and years working at their respective crafts, enduring rejection, unreturned phone calls, working in jobs they hate to make ends meet until by sheer luck born of desperate perseverance the door finally opens.

In truth the dedication and focus required to forge any kind of career in Hollywood is monumental, with the years of humiliation encountered on the way resulting in a damaged soul regardless.

But, again, I digress.

With one of my scripts now in development, I'd managed to push the door open a little. Now, where before I could not see any hope of my circumstances ever changing, I felt positive about the future, waiting expectantly for that call to come through from Tom or Jack at any minute informing me that such and such a name director or actor had read the script and wanted to be involved in the project. I took to calling Tom every week for a progress report. I liked him at first; he was funny, street wise, always cracking jokes in his heavy New York accent, one redolent of your stereotypical, tough talking Hollywood producer. Jack, his partner, was a different kind of character altogether. From an affluent background back in the UK, he had gone to Oxford before coming out to LA on a student exchange to work as an intern for one of the big production outfits, starting at the bottom and working his way up. He was clever, phlegmatic, but most importantly a gentleman, destined for big things according to those who knew and/or had worked with him.

Their office was located directly across the street from the massive Sony studio lot in Culver City, and quite often I would drive down there for meetings. It was a good time, the best I'd experienced since arriving here, when I began to believe that everything might just work out and it would all fall into place.

11

But then two passenger aircraft slammed into the twin towers of the World Trade Center to change the course of history.

I recall that it was just after 11 in the morning when the phone woke me up. I'd worked through to the early hours the previous night at a bar/restaurant across the other side of town in Brentwood. The place drew a young, raucous crowd of mostly students from the vast UCLA campus in nearby Westwood. Most of them were white and most of them were the product of rich parents - at least if the clothes they wore, the cars they pulled up in, and the arrogant, cocksure manner in which they carried themselves were anything to go by. The place was popular, packed most nights, and I'd recently begun working there a few nights a week. By the time my shift ended at around three in the morning and I'd completed the half-hour drive back to

Hollywood, it was always with a sense of relief that I hit the light and fell into bed.

Anyway, on this particular morning the phone wrenched me awake. I'll never forget Gabriel's first words when I reached over and picked it up: 'Switch on the TV! We're under attack!'

The fact Gabriel had said '*We're* under attack', despite the fact he was from Sweden, did not strike me as strange at the time. I was half asleep and if you knew Gabriel you'd know him as someone who'd embraced America and its culture with the zeal of a new convert.

Anyway, I did as he instructed and literally could not believe my eyes. I'd missed the first aircraft hitting one of the towers of the World Trade Center, but the news networks were replaying it over and over. Then, fifteen minutes or so later, along with the millions watching on TV live around the world the world, I sat stupefied as another aircraft slammed into the second tower.

Stunned, numb, amazed - words don't come close to

describing the mixed emotions I experienced, experiencing them one after the other in rapid-fire sequence.

In the the next hour or two, watching news footage of people jumping to a gruesome death from the towers, both of which were belching fire and smoke, then of the towers collapsing into mountains of dust and rubble, hearing the reports of the number of police and firemen who'd lost their lives attempting to rescue people, I was filled with horror at the extent of the human catastrophe unfolding before my eyes.

Then I felt afraid, scared of what would now come by way of retaliation. If there was one thing that set the United States apart from other nations, it was its willingness to unleash violence on a massive scale against any nation or people that dared stand in its way or do it harm. Whoever was responsible for this atrocity - not just on the World Trade Center, but also by this point on the Pentagon - had just signed their own death warrant, along with that of their country if it turned out that a state or government was in any way involved.

News coverage of the attack was blanket for the next few days. All the news networks crammed their schedules with military experts, political analysts and a plethora of commentators. In those first few days after 9/11 you really got a sense of nation having just been rocked back on its heels. Comparisons were drawn with the attack on Pearl Harbor, which had spawned America's entry into the Second World War. Congressmen and women from both political parties joined hands outside the Capitol Building to sing *God Bless America*. Meanwhile, messages of condolence for the victims, along with offers of assistance, poured in from all over the world. Even Cuban president Fidel Castro, whose country had endured a decades-long economic embargo by the United States, sent a message of solidarity and an offer of help in the shape of Cuban doctors and medical professionals.

On the front page of *Le Monde*, France's newspaper of record, the next day's headline read: 'We Are All Americans'. In London, for the first time in history, royal protocol was set aside and instead of *God Save the Queen* being played at the annual Trooping the Colour ceremony to honour the Queen, the band struck up *The Star-Spangled Banner* in tribute to the American people.

The president, George 'Dubya' Bush, re-emerged from a secret hideout somewhere in Ohio three days later. His initial statements and press conferences were subdued. It was obvious that the administration was unsure about the line to take or the the tone to adopt as the nation and the entire world waited with baited breath. What was going to happen now?

Reporters and journalists started asking the questions that were on everybody's lips. Who may have been responsible for this? Al Qaeda, Saddam - who?

Investigations were ongoing. This is all the administration would say.

The streets around Hollywood, normally teeming with traffic on weekend nights, were eerily quiet. Even the Sunset Strip was dead, the flashing neon reminiscent now of some abandoned theme park. Most people were paralyzed with shock, with many too numb to be able to discuss it with anything approaching coherence. The rage and calls for revenge, the unvaunted patriotism, had yet to materialize in those first few days.

Interestingly, there were some people I spoke to in the aftermath of 9/11 who offered an opinion that was at odds with the deluge of condemnation and patriotism which the atrocity unleashed. The attendant at the parking lot where I parked my car every night was one of them. Originally from Mexico, he and I had got into the habit of exchanging a few words whenever I passed in and out on the way to and from my car. A day or so after the attack took place I passed him as usual and the first thing he said was, 'You see what happens, senor? You see what happens when you go around the world bombing and killing people?'

But there was one individual I spoke to who stood out with the passionate and radical nature of his views. Originally from Ghana, Walter's position, which he stated without hesitation or apology, was that America had received its just desserts. I'd met Walter a couple of weeks before 9/11 at the bar in Brentwood, in which unbeknown to me he was an investor. Our first encounter was in the form of a confrontation, during which heated words were exchanged when he tried to barge his way in ahead of the queue of people who'd been waiting patiently outside. I prevented him and we started arguing.

He said his piece and I said mine and that was the end of it. The following weekend, just after 9/11, he came back into the place and approached me smiling with his hand outstretched. We shook hands and he apologized for the earlier incident. He then went on to say how much he admired the Irish people for fighting for their freedom against the British. I didn't get the chance to point out that I was in fact Scottish because he went straight into a rant denouncing Britain and the United States for their crimes against the African people, their colonization of the Middle East, and so on. He became increasingly passionate and excited, to the point where I felt uncomfortable listening to him.

I took him over to the side and tried to calm him down. Walter was an angry man with strong opinions on everything from America's role in the world to how he was being cheated by his partners and fellow investors at the club. It was obvious to me that he was damaged goods.

Finally, and I have to say thankfully, he said his goodbyes and left. The manager came up to me immediately afterwards and declared that Walter was an idiot, that nobody liked him, and that the only reason he was so pissed off was that he'd made and lost a fortune in failed business venture after failed business venture.

Yet there was something about Walter I liked at first, despite his anger and paranoia over how he was being mistreated and persecuted by the world. I think it was the manner in which he wore his heart on his sleeve and spoke his mind without fear or favour. He lived in a luxury penthouse apartment in West Hollywood, sharing it with his business partner, whom he claimed was also cheating him. They were in the process of setting up a business manufacturing health food supplements. Walter was providing the money, his partner the idea and know-how required to make it work.

As I got to know him more, he revealed that he made his fortune selling marijuana. In the end, tired of the stress involved, he got out with close to a million dollars in cash to invest. However, rather than invest the money wisely, he proceeded to hand it over to assorted friends and acquaintances on the basis of some very ropey business ideas. None of them proved successful and within a year his money had dwindled to the point where he was on the brink of going broke. Along with his fortune went his friends, who all abandoned him. Now he was left pinning his last hope of financial redemption on his current project to manufacture a new line in health food supplements.

I never got a chance to see how things worked out for Walter, as after a while I found him just too sensitive and brittle to be around. He hated the world and everyone in it, and he had little compunction in letting people know. Rather than a man who spoke freely, as I'd initially thought, I realized instead that he was simply lacking in manners and respect for others. His story was a lesson in how an obsession with money will destroy you. You may live in a luxury apartment, drive a nice car and wear expensive clothes, but what's the point if the end product is a bitter and miserable human being?

I remember our last conversation. Walter called me up one evening to inform me that he was going to shoot Gabriel. Why? It turned out Gabriel had committed the cardinal sin of refusing to let him and his friends into a bar he was working at in Hollywood the previous night. Even though I thought he was just letting off steam, I called Gabriel to warn him nonetheless. Gabriel laughed it off, saying that Walter was just full of shit and that if he had a dollar for every time somebody threatened him on the door he'd be a millionaire.

It appeared he was right as Walter never showed up at the bar again. A month or so later, at home watching the news on TV, suddenly Walter's face popped up. He'd been arrested for shooting his business partner Gary.

12

It wasn't long after 9/11 - six weeks or thereabouts - that I joined the antiwar movement. By then it was already apparent that the Bush administration, not content with bombing and occupying Afghanistan, was intent on using 9/11 as a pretext to do the same to Iraq. I decided it was impossible to sit back and do nothing in the face of what would certainly involve the loss of life on a grand scale, expecially when the devastation already inflicted on Iraq and the Iraqi people during a decade of sanctions after the first gulf war in 1991 had constituted a crime against humanity. According to the UN, over 2 million Iraqis had died as a direct result of these sanctions, over half a million of those children under the age of five. Medical equipment, basic medicines, food, clean water - all of these basic essentials and more had been deprived a nation whose people at one point enjoyed the highest living standards of any in the region. Sanctions designed to hurt Saddam Hussein had instead only served to stabilize his power base by handing his regime the responsibility of being the sole distributor of food, thus ensuring that opposition from within became well-nigh impossible. Moreover, in time the Iraqi people turned their anger away from their government and onto the Western powers that had placed them under this state of siege, one so cruel it was positively medieval.

Madeleine Albright, Secretary of State in the Clinton administration, when asked during a TV interview in 1996 if the deaths of half a million Iraqi children under the sanctions was a price worth paying to punish Saddam, had infamously replied 'yes'. The case for war against Iraq being put forward by the Bush administration nine years later consisted of claims that in contravention of previous UN resolutions, Saddam still possessed weapons of mass destruction, chemical and biological, weapons that he'd already used against the Kurds in the northern Iraq and weapons he could supply to terrorists intent on attacking the US and/or US interests around the globe. Efforts were already underway to associate Saddam with Bin Laden and Al Qaeda, even though they were sworn ideological enemies - Saddam being a secular nationalist and Bin Laden an Islamic fundamentalist.

As US and Western governments have done throughout history in order to justify attacking countries and regimes they disapprove of, Saddam was demonized, portrayed in the media as evil incarnate, a monster constituting a threat to the future of humanity no less. It was a ploy that worked a charm on huge swathes of the American people, who unsurprisingly were angry, scared and malleable as a result of the attack on their country.

I first learned of the existence of the ANSWER Coalition while driving north on La Brea one sunny afternoon on my way back from yet another wretched stint as an extra on some TV show or other. I was listening to the local progressive radio station, KPFK, part of the Pacifica Network which operates a chain of progressive radio stations throughout the US, to help take my mind off the nose-to-tail traffic. I listened to KPFK most of the time in the car, if only to get a different perspective and analysis of the news and events. It was a station funded exclusively by listener donations, providing it with the freedom and latitude to offer an alternative to the corporate-controlled mainstream crap which colonized the airwaves. My attention was drawn to an announcement advertising a public meeting on the looming war against Iraq. It gave out the phone number of the organization involved, which I quickly scribbled down with the intention of calling later. When I did I got this guy on the phone. His name was Frank and we spoke briefly. He sounded friendly as he gave me the address, driving directions, and the date and time of the next meeting.

For some time now I'd been reading the works of political commentators, historians, radical journalists and thinkers. I'd thought and pondered on my direction in life, on all the received and previously closely-held truths I'd been inculcated with as a product of the environment in which I'd grown up, gradually stripping them away one by one to reveal me increasingly angry at the injustice, inequality, greed, venality, and out-and-out barbarism of the economic and social system which liberal democracy had spawned.

It isn't easy holding beliefs and convictions that are at odds with most of the people you come into contact with. The conversations among extras on Hollywood movies and TV shows had become harder and harder listen to much less participate in. The mundane day to day concerns of how to get an agent, a SAG card, a line on a movie or a TV show, how to book a commercial, filled me with revulsion. Didn't these people realize what was going on around them? Didn't they understand that they were being fucked on a daily basis? What was wrong with them? And yet just two years previously, arriving in LA, I too had been consumed with getting ahead in Hollywood. But now, though still working with Tom and Jack to get one of my scripts produced, my heart was no longer in it. I'd spent weeks doing rewrites and rushing down to their office to hand-deliver each new improved draft, in the process allowing my hopes to be built up by the possibilities painted by the two of them.

That they were extremely dedicated, hard-working and determined to succeed was unquestionable. Periodically, they would inform me that so-and-so had indicated an interest in the project, some well-known director or actor; of how it was already in the hands of Miramax, New Line, or some other mega production company. Tom had sent me out on a couple of what's referred to in the business as 'general' meetings.

These take place after a certain producer has read and appreciated your work and decides that you might be worth getting to know just you in case you might, by some fluke, write something they might wish to get involved with further on down the line.

People in general responded positively to the script, but not and never enough to commit to it with a fee or to commission me to write something on the strength of it.

In short, it was all just a game, a piece of theater with a cast of thousands. Every day in Hollywood hundreds of such meetings take place, involving a desperate writer who hopes that in the five or ten minutes allotted they are able to impress a jaded and cynical producer enough to actually and at last, after years of fruitless toil, pay them to write something they hate. Any notion of writing films that might move people, which carried a strong message about society and the human condition, had been knocked out of me by Tom, a man for whom the word philistine was undoubtedly invented.

'Listen,' he said to me one day over a sandwich at a deli close to his office, a three-dollar sandwich and a cup of coffee constituting his idea of the lunch he'd promised to take me on for the past few weeks in order to talk over my work. 'Listen,' he said. 'Forget about writing stories about poor people, homeless people, social injustice, an' shit like that. This is fuckin' Hollywood. People wanna see stories that make 'em feel good…that excite and entertain 'em.

'What I want you to do from now on is scour the paper every day. Pick out stories you think have a movie in them, run 'em by me, and I'll tell ya whether or not ya got something. Stop wasting your time and start thinkin' big. What sells, that's what you should be thinkin'. This business is all about grabbing a chunk of studio money. Everything else is bullshit.'

As he spoke the Rolex Submariner on his wrist gleamed under a coruscating midday sun. Every second guy on the make in LA seemed to have one of these monstrosities on their wrist, a vulgar and obscene manifestation of everything that was ugly about this town. In my experience they marked the owner out as a contrived human being before they even got a chance to open their mouth. And in this assertion I was never wrong.

The point is I no longer believed in what I was doing. My political consciousness was growing, with the result that I felt myself being pulled in a different direction altogether.

The 'answer' in ANSWER Coaliton was and is an acronym of Act Now to Stop War and End Racism. With branches in most major cities across the United States, and headquarters in New York, ANSWER was formed immediately after 9/11 by a Marxist-Leninist organization called the Workers World Party, or WWP. The coalition also included the Free Palestine Alliance - as the name suggests an organization committed to the Palestinian struggle - the Haiti Support Network, Mexico Solidarity Network, along with various other organizations the name of which have since receded from memory. ANSWER also worked closely with the National Lawyers Guild, a group of lawyers and attorneys formed during the Great Depression in the 1930s with a proud history of supporting progressive and left-wing causes. Their members were distinctive in their yellow baseball caps at demonstrations, where they monitored the actions of the police to make sure they did not violate the civil rights of those demonstrating.

The group's figurehead was the controversial lawyer, Ramsey Clark, a former Attorney General in the Johnson administration back in the late sixties at the height of the war in Vietnam. Clark had been radicalized by the war and the callous disregard for the massive loss of life being suffered by the Vietnamese people on the part of the US government. He later recounted how each day the president and his cabinet would meet at the White House to discuss the war and how racist epithets were liberally bandied around by everyone in the room, including the president, when talking about the Vietnamese. Clark grew so disgusted and disenchanted by this that he turned his back on Washington and the US establishment to embark on a new career fighting on behalf of radical causes.

ANSWER'S LA office was situated in the heart of Korea Town,

halfway down Western Avenue. I attended my first meeting there one bright but untypically cool Saturday afternoon. Following the directions I'd been given on the phone, I made my way over, parked the car in a quiet side street off the main drag, and walked across the street to their office. It was one in a suite of offices housed in the same building. I only knew I'd come to the right place by the poster that was stuck on the window facing the street. It was a poster of Mumia al Jumal, a black activist and journalist who was in prison for allegedly gunning down a police officer in Philadelphia. He'd been sentenced to death for the killing, despite compelling evidence pointing to the possibility that he'd been set up by the police. His case had become something of a cause célèbre not just in the US but internationally among progressives.

As ever, due to the LA traffic, I arrived late. Rather sheepishly, I took a vacant seat at the back of the room, directed there by a guy who introduced himself with a whisper as Frank, the very same I'd originally spoken to over the phone. The meeting was on the current situation in the Middle East and the speaker soon had my rapt attention with words such as imperialism and hegemony pouring forth. I would guess there were about fifteen people in the audience, of all ages and ethnicity, and in no time I felt completely at ease, like a man who'd just discovered his place in the world.

The speaker had travelled down from San Francisco to address the meeting specially. His name was Ralph, I was to hear him speak many times after this initial meeting, and his knowledge and analysis of events would never fail to impress me. He ended his speech, which lasted around forty minutes, to enthusiastic applause. The meeting was then opened up to questions and contributions from the floor. Half a dozen hands went up and a lively discussion ensued.

I became distracted at a certain point by the surroundings. The walls were covered with posters celebrating historical events such as the Russian and Cuban revolutions, along with historical figures such as Trotsky, Lenin, and Che Guevara. Bookshelves ran the length of each wall and were crammed with titles on every revolutionary movement and by every revolutionary leader and thinker who'd ever lived. I had to remind myself that I was still in the most capitalist city of the most capitalist country on the planet, though self-evidently one in which people were still able to hold and disseminate radical ideas.

After the meeting ended, Frank came over and properly introduced himself. He then introduced me to Peter, Joe Park, and Milly, the core organizers within the branch. Lastly I was introduced to Ralph himself. Upon learning that I was from the UK he began plying me with questions as to the political situation over there. Everyone at the meeting without exception made me feel most welcome; this in contrast to the few other political meetings I'd attended up to that point, where I'd picked up an aura of suspicion and detachment among those present which had left me feeling less than welcome.

They invited me to lunch at a café along the street. I was delighted to accept and spent the next couple of hours engrossed in conversation about radical politics and the prospects of war being unleashed on Iraq. By the time we parted company my head was reeling. It was a feeling hard to describe, but I was stimulated and inspired to such an extent that on the drive back to Hollywood I resolved to get involved.

Fast forward two weeks and there I am, attending my first event as volunteer with the ANSWER Coalition in the form of a march and rally against the Bush administration's march to war. The venue was a patch of grass adjacent to the Federal Building on Wilshire Boulevard in Westwood, where the march was scheduled to begin and end with speeches. I'd been designated to work as one of the stewards on the march and it was with a sense of purpose that I arrived and checked in with Peter and the rest of the group at the ANSWER stall. Speaking of stalls, the thing that immediately struck me upon arrival was the sheer number of them offering a myriad of magazines, pamphlets, books, badges, bumper sticker and T-shirts. There was literature covering feminism, LGBT rights, anarchism, environmentalism, animal rights – on every left-wing or progressive cause you care to name. Stall after stall announcing the presence of different parties and organizations was my introduction to the factionalism that has traditionally beset the left and progressive movement. Most of the different groups represented were so small in number it was risible, yet each was absolutely convinced of the correctness of their own particular line and analysis of both historical and current events.

Peter directed me to stand at the side of the flatbed truck that was being used as the stage for the speakers. My role was to ensure that nobody attempted to get up on the truck who wasn't supposed to. Anonymous threats had been made against the demo Peter informed me by people offended at the movement's support for the Palestinian struggle in particular, and he cited past incidents where groups or individuals had sought to disrupt demonstrations. As mentioned, one of the groups in the coalition was the Free Palestine Alliance, devoted to the struggle to end Israel's occupation and the colonization of Palestinian land. Their commitment to the Palestinian struggle was laudable in a society so overwhelmingly pro-Israel.

The opening rally lasted around half an hour. Afterwards, everyone formed up behind the truck and the lead banner for a march through the streets of Westwood. The truck crawled along behind a five or six police patrol cars, with people on the truck leading chants through the PA system.

We marched for about a mile. Shoppers and pedestrians stopped to watch as we passed with drums beating and banners flying. Most of them appeared nonplussed, as if they were looking at a parade of circus freaks. A few clapped or shouted messages of support. There wasn't, I noticed, any significant opposition to our message - or at least not overt opposition. The number and range of banners on the march was impressive. They succeeded in giving the impression that the march was bigger than it really was.

Finally, after marching for around forty minutes, we arrived back where we started. Here more speakers addressed the crowd, which by this point had dwindled considerably. I was tired; the heat had taken its toll and by this point I was thinking of a shower and a long, cool drink. At last the rally came to a close and everyone began to pack up. I helped pack away the ANSWER stall and materials before parting company with the others and heading for my car, parked a short walk away on Wilshire. As I walked I thought about the short exchange I'd just had with Peter and Frank. Having asked me what I thought about the event, I told them that I thought it was pretty small but that it made up for the lack of numbers with lots of colour and noise. I didn't say anything at the time, but I was taken aback when they estimated the crowd to have been somewhere in the region of five thousand people. You were lucky if there was a third of that number present and I couldn't understand how they could arrive at such an inflated figure, or indeed anything like it.

I was to learn in the months and years to come that this was common practice within the movement, the overestimation of numbers at demonstrations and rallies. While the authorities always made it their business to underestimate numbers, we always did the opposite. In time I would be doing the same without as much as a second's thought.

From that day on I was in the ANSWER office most days, answering the phone, sorting through the mail, helping to update the database, and carrying out any other tasks that needed doing. Frank was the only full-time volunteer in the branch and so it was from him that I received my political orientation and initial education into the organization's doctrine and philosophy.

Day after day in the office, just the two of us, we discussed politics, the ongoing situation in the Middle East, and all the great revolutions and social movements that had gone before. As I said, I already knew that the core group within the coalition was comprised of members of the Workers World Party, and I was interested in learning more. When I offered my opinion while talking to Frank one day that the Soviet Union hadn't really been a socialist state, that it had been in fact a dictatorship in which the masses were oppressed, he disagreed. The WWP had a policy of not criticizing socialist countries over their flaws and distortions, he explained.

The same applied to nations of the developing world that were deemed enemies of the West, including those ruled by dictatorships. Instead, the Party considered its role to help these countries develop by getting the US off their backs. The state of all socialist countries past and present, he maintained, was down to the pressure exerted on them by the US and the West in the form of capitalist encirclement. Furthermore, he went on, most of the slander levelled at the former Soviet Union, China and Cuba was nothing more than propaganda, its aim to discredit socialism and socialist ideas.

When I asked him about lack of democracy in the aforementioned states, he made the point that liberal democracy was responsible for more inequality, poverty, hunger, war and carnage than any political system there'd ever been. He cited the slave trade, the untold millions of people who'd died as a result under colonialism, the First and Second World Wars, global poverty, the six million children who perished every year in the developing world as a result of hunger and preventable disease, and the despoliation of the environment to prove his point. All were consequences of capitalism and liberal democracy, its political face. What liberalism had done in truth, he said, was equate inequality, both internally between classes and externally between nations, with civilization. He then hit me with a list of books I should read on the subject. Most of them were available at the office and I took a couple to pore over at home.

Peter worked as a male nurse at a medical clinic in downtown LA. Without fail he came straight to the office every day after his shift ended. He was aged somewhere in his mid-to late-fifties and had been active in politics from his days at college in Arkansas, where he was from. He was very much the driving force behind the inclusion of LGBT issues as part and parcel of the various causes the group was involved in. I liked Peter; he was warm, charismatic, approachable, and out of everyone he commanded the most respect both within and without the coalition among the wider progressive community. Within the branch there was not supposed to be one leader but rather a collective leadership; however, in LA Peter had undoubtedly assumed the mantle of de facto leader. People came to him before going to anyone else, attracted to his personable nature and friendly demeanour.

Joe Park and Milly were a couple. Joe was black, extremely knowledgeable theoretically but without either Peter's charm or Frank's skills as an organizer. He was the driving force behind the organization's work in support of the black community; its struggle against poverty and the regular incidents of police brutality its members were subjected to. Milly was in charge of the group's finances. She was very quiet and hard to get to know in the beginning. However, this quiet, almost shy exterior belied someone whose commitment to the aims of the organization was total and consumed every fibre of her being.

Below the organizers in the scheme of things were the active volunteers, some of whom, like me, had become involved in the wake of 9/11. There was Ivor and Mandy, Rob, Hank, Rudy, Mirko and Alan, along with various others. Out of them all Rudy stood out. In his late sixties, he was all passion and fire and a joy to be around. Originally from Algeria, he'd served in the French Army and had spent ten years living in Paris, where he became an ardent communist. In the US, where he'd lived for over forty years, he'd been active in the CPUSA (Communist Party of the

United States), remaining true to his principles and beliefs throughout. I loved listening to his many stories from his years as an activist while living in the belly of the beast.

Ivor was a young lawyer from a background of comfort and privilege. He was very bright, idealistic and driven. His partner Mandy was a Palestinian born and educated in the United States. Unsurpringly, she held a deep attachment to the Palestinian struggle, which meant she was very much at home within the movement. Like Ivor she was a lawyer and together they appeared the perfect couple. As for Hank, he was one hundred percent Texan. With his booming voice, loud shirts and cowboy hat, he bounded in and out like the blue collar guy he most certainly was. Unlike most of the main activists he was neither a socialist or a Marxist. Nor was he remotely interested in becoming one. He was a proud American who believed in the Constitution and the history of what he viewed as a great country. He hated George Bush and the Republicans with a passion, and it seemed to me his politics were more suited to Ralph Nader and the Green Party than a coalition behind which the main drivers were people that believed in class struggle and revolution.

Mirko and Alan were Iranian and had come to the movement together. Both were committed Marxist-Leninists before they arrived. They were outspoken and critical of how things were done. The result was that in a short period of time they succeeded in alienating many of the other activists, not to mention the leadership. In time, however, some of their criticisms of the methods and tactics employed by the group would prove valid.

This then was the LA branch of the ANSWER Coalition as I found it when I joined around the beginning of October 2001. We came from different backgrounds and all walks of life, drawn by events and by a seed of consciousness that had grown to the point where political inactivity had become impossible. At the time if anyone had bothered to ask what motivated me to put all my spare time into political activism I would have struggled to provide a suitable response. However, years later I would read a passage in an old, secondhand book I came across that articulated the answer better than I ever could. The book, *An American Testament*, was written in the late 1930s by Joseph Freeman. In the book he writes:

> *"When you don't see what is right and what is true, you are free to follow your little egotistical interests. You can chase after money and women and glory. But when you do see the right thing, you must either fight for it or go to pieces. If you don't see the truth you are merely blind. But if you see it and do not support it, you become corrupt."*

This passage, I believe, accurately describes the drive that lies within those committed to the struggle for justice and who dedicate themselves to political activism regardless of the personal cost to themselves.

13

A day of national demonstration against the impending war on Iraq had been called to take place at the end of October 2002. There were events planned - one in Washington DC and one in San Francisco. Our focus was helping to build the demo in San Francisco by running as many buses from LA as we could fill. It was hoped and expected that tens of thousands would converge from cities and towns the length and breadth of the western half of the country and we were determined to play our part.

As the date approached the office became increasingly busy. Every time you walked in, at any hour of the day or evening, you entered a hive of frenetic activity: people writing text for leaflets and other campaign literature, others fielding and making phone calls, others huddled together to discuss a specific aspect of the mobilization, with still others making banners. Meetings at the office which attracted twenty to twenty-five people just a few weeks before now drew in sixty or more on a near nightly basis. People were getting angry at what was happening, and more and more were channeling their anger into doing something about it.

Describe the Bush administration as execrable and loathsome to most of these people and you would have found yourself pilloried for being soft. George W Bush had come to power on the back of an election that was covered in controversy back in 2000. Allegations of vote rigging and voter registration fraud hadn't gone away, and it was commonly felt that Bush's victory in that election was the result of illegality. People were angry that nothing had been done about it, that such practices could stand in what they believed to be the world's foremost democracy.

Among activists from a variety of backgrounds, ethnicities, and cultures, there were bound to be differences of analysis and political orientation. Most I found retained their belief in the US system of governance, the Constitution and the economic system, and felt that Bush was an aberration that just needed to be removed for all to be right in the world again.

This wasn't the view of people like Peter, Frank or any of the other core organizers and activists in the branch. They viewed the Bush administration as an extreme manifestation of an economic system predicated on profit regardless of the social or human cost. The US ruling class comprised Republicans and Democrats alike; and you only had to look back through history to see that Democratic Party administrations had embarked on more wars of occupation and aggression than their Republican counterparts; this despite the Republicans being traditionally considered the pro-war party of the two.

Capitalism to them was an economic system which must constantly grow or else stagnate and collapse. At the point where the domestic market is satiated, capitalist economies look outwith their own borders for the profits they so desperately need. Where this economic expansion and capitalist penetration is blocked by those nations intent on protecting their sovereignty and/or the welfare of their own people, military power is used to smash open the door and assert control over natural resources and new markets. Historically, when rival capitalist powers compete for markets, natural resources and colonies, the result has been war, with the two World Wars prime examples. After the Second World War the capitalist world accepted the unrivalled leadership of the United States, whose economy had emerged significantly stronger, while the likes of France, Germany and Britain emerged from the war with their respective economies in ruins.

The result was that only the Soviet Union rivalled the US in terms of global hegemony in the postwar decades. The ensuing Cold War, lasting from the end of the Second World War to the Soviet Union's collapse in 1991, had acted as a check on both. But now, with the US the world's sole superpower, in the wake of 9/11 the Bush administration was intent on exploiting this power to secure a *Pax Americana*. In the famous words of the Roman historian Tacitus, which he attributed to the last of the barbarian chiefs, Calgagus, to resist Rome's power over ancient Britain, *'They make a desert and they call it peace'*.

The Bush administration was using the atrocity of 9/11 as a pretext, an excuse to carry out their strategic goals in the Middle East: namely control of Iraq's vast reserves of oil. Iraq had absolutely nothing to do with 9/11, yet still the likes Condoleezza Rice, Colin Powell, Donald Rumsfeld, and of course the President himself, attempted to draw a connection. It was as shameful as it was repugnant to watch and listen to them repeating lie after lie in this regard, at the same time disheartening to see the near complete lack of questioning or probing by the mainstream media in response.

Based on the depth of their analysis, along with their unshakable conviction and determination, I found myself draw closer to the core group as the days and weeks passed. What impressed me most about them was their resolute refusal to buckle under the weight of the mountain of propaganda vilifying those nations and regimes that the US painted as dictatorships or repressive. Instead they applied the principle of cause and effect to explain the reasons why certain regimes in the developing world had developed in the way they had, a direct result of US-led western pressure to destabilize and undermine them in pursuit of global hegemony and the spread of the free market to every corner of the globe.

As the day of the San Francisco demonstration drew closer, in line with the escalating military build up in the Middle East, we found ourselves literally deluged with calls and emails from people trying to book places on the buses we were organizing. The initial objective of filling ten buses was soon surpassed, until with a week to go over twenty had been booked in order to satisfy the demand. The atmosphere in the office was electric, like something I'd never experienced, born of a belief I think that what we were involved in was truly historic and that the objective of stopping the war before it began was achievable.

The veterans within the branch were especially thrilled at the massive upsurge in political activity that was taking place. Peter for example could trace his political activity all the way back to the anti-Vietnam War struggle. He had stuck with it through thick and thin in the years since. To see it suddenly explode in such dramatic fashion had infused him with newfound hope.

Deciding that I would fly up to San Francisco rather than take the bus in order to take advantage of an offer to stay with an ex-girlfriend Connie for the weekend, I arrived there on the Thursday night, whereupon I spent that night and all the next day getting reacquainted with a city I had grown to love in the few short months I'd spent there a few years prior. Connie and I had met while we were both on holiday in South Beach, Miami a few years previously. We'd enjoyed a brief if intense relationship thereafter, during which I spent a few months living with her in San Franciso. But while my affection for her may have dimmed in time, my affection for San Francisco had continued unabated. Consequently, the opportunity to revisit old haunts - cafés, bookstores, bars - in North Beach, Chinatown, and downtown was just too good to pass up.

It is often the case you don't realize how much you've changed or evolved until you come into contact with someone you haven't seen in years. When I was with Connie four years previously I may have called myself a communist, but I was one who was happy to remain inactive. I recall dragging her along to a couple of meetings way down in the bowels of the Mission District, a low income part of the city mainly populated by immigrants from Central and South America. There, in a run down office, she would sit alongside me at a table with around half a dozen other people, forced to listen to a long exposition of the *Communist Manifesto* or other Marxist tracts. I only knew she was bored shitless because I was. This, I should explain, was a woman who liked the finer things in life - expensive clothes, wine, and food - and sitting in that pokey wee office, she was definitely out of place.

I only went to a few of those meetings, deciding in the end that changing the world could wait. Connie and I would sometimes talk about politics, but it was a topic that often ended in argument, to the point where I learned to leave it alone. From Mexico, she of course knew what poverty was. But she'd been fortunate to have been left a substantial sum of money by her maternal grandmother when she died. Connie used it to travel the world for the next few years, visiting Europe and other far flung places, shopping, skiing, and living it up in nightclubs and restaurants with a succession of boyfriends.

Disappointingly, after spending just a day together prior to the demo, it was clear that our paths had diverged too much for us to even remain friends. After years working as a waitress in various high-class restaurants around the city, she had succeeded in getting a job as a buyer for a prestigious wine distributor. The job involved her touring vineyards and wineries all over Europe, staying in first-class hotels and mixing with people with money. It had infused her with an outlook on life that was the antithesis of my own. As for the upcoming demonstration, she could not have been more disparaging, referring to those involved as 'losers' and 'idiots'.

Meanwhile, the news was not good with regard to Iraq, with the Bush administration's rhetoric growing increasingly bellicose. Not content with bombing the shit out of Afghanistan, they were now claiming that Saddam possessed a secret arsenal of chemical and biological weapons and was intent on developing a nuclear weapons programme, demanding that he open up his country to inspections. The overwhelming consensus within the movement was that Bush and members of his administration were lying through their teeth; that all this talk of WMD was merely a pretext for carrying out the economic and strategic objective of asserting control over Iraq's oil reserves by toppling Saddam and putting in his place a pliant regime.

On the morning of the demo, I was up at the crack of dawn. Connie was still fast asleep when I left.

The walk down Pacific in the direction of Chinatown was every bit as magnificent as I remembered. The view of Alcatraz and the Bay to the left could not have been more spectacular. It was offset by a brilliant blue sky and a cool breeze which filled me with gladness.

Chinatown was its usual cornucopia of madness and mayhem, its streets packed with people going about their business to create a din of activity that has to be experienced to be believed. Nowhere in the city could you find better food and a warmer welcome than here.

Passing through Chinatown you entered North Beach, where San Francisco's Italian heritage is celebrated. The cafes, restaurants, and bars here are packed every weekend, and I'd lost count of the hours I had spent sitting outside the cafes here sipping a piping hot latte while watching the world go by. With a few hours to kill before the demo began, I did exactly that now, ordering myself not just a latte but a large plate of scrambled eggs on wheat toast to help fortify me for the long day ahead.

An hour later, I was on my way again, headed in the direction of Market Street and the demo assembly point. As I got closer I began to see more and more see protesters milling around. Some were carrying banners and placards, and most had on T-shirts, hats, badges or sweatshirts carrying a political message. I saw many 'Che' T-shirts and flags carrying that universally known iconic image by Alberto Korda, Che's face a picture of the unflinching determination, strength and conviction with which he will forever be associated.

By now it had gone just after eleven and reaching the assembly point the number of people converging from every direction was staggering. A veritable flood of humanity was arriving and my initial excitement gave way to a state of barely-suppressed euphoria. It was going to be massive.

And it was.

By the time it came for the march to set off there was so many people you couldn't move in any direction. Speeches were being given by speakers standing on the back of a flat-bed truck. From where I was standing you could hardly hear a word, despite the fact they were using a PA system. Flags and banners, placards and signs of every description were flying. Some of the slogans were funny, some clever, others both.

Stalls by the hundred where you could buy T-shirts, literature, badges, hats etc. peppered the street. People were out hawking all manner of left-wing newspapers and pamphlets, representing a multitude of progressive causes and organizations. There were people identifying themselves as anarchists, socialists, Marxists, Marxist-Leninists, Maoists, anarcho-syndicalists, environmentalists, and so on. Labor unions were represented, as were religious organizations of all faiths; however, the vast bulk of the crowd was made up of ordinary people who felt compelled to raise their voices against the Bush administration's march to war. They were of every ethnicity, age, demographic and background and their diversity was a powerful symbol of resistance to the polarizing policies of their own government, leaving you with the sense that a struggle was underway for the future of humanity.

Peter had told me before leaving LA to find him and the others at the front of the march, which it was arranged volunteers from the LA branch would be stewarding. With some effort I managed to squeeze my way through the vast crowd to the front just before the march set off. Peter and the others were there and I quickly joined them.

The march began with a deafening roar and began rolling along the entire length of Market Street. At one point I looked round to get an idea of its size and was met by a mass of people stretching way back as far as the eye could see. Some groups were shouting slogans as they went, others singing, while still more were dancing to music, creating a mood that was more celebratory than angry. The war hadn't begun and people felt they really could stop it if they just came out and demonstrated in sufficient numbers. You couldn't blame them given the atmosphere and numbers that were present.

By the time the front of the march reached the huge square adjacent to City Hall, where a massive stage and sound system had been set up to accommodate a long list of speakers, news was filtering through that the sister march in Washington was even bigger than ours, with half a million people being announced from the stage and the crowd erupting in response. Surely now they won't be able to ignore us was the consensus among those in attendance.

Speaker after speaker took to the stage to address the crowd. Most of them repeated what had already been said by the previous speaker, and after a while my interest waned and I went on a wander round the multitude of stalls that were set up.

It had the effect of dampening my spirits. Unity, I was learning fast, was a word from another language with regard to the left and progressive politics. There was no need for most of these groups to exist independently of one another; especially not when faced with a government intent on ushering in a regressive period on the back of an agenda of war and militarism. Combatting this agenda would require that any opposition be coherent and unified. However, the fragmentation, suspicion and sectarianism I'd already witnessed and heard from too many told me that there was still a long way to go before anything like a truly united movement was possible.

I stayed at the rally for forty minutes of so, long enough to hear people like Martin Sheen, Tim Robbins, and Susan Sarandon speak. They were all very good, voicing principled and impassioned arguments against the drive to war. I admired the fact they were willing to speak despite the very real danger of their stance resulting in them being blacklisted in Hollywood. A repressive chill in the air was already present within the industry, which many commentators were comparing to the dark days of McCarthyism. This made it doubly important that Hollywood actors and celebrities, like the aforementioned trio, spoke out. Hopefully it would encourage others to do the same and create a momentum.

Washington had always feared Hollywood, feared the influence it had over people not only living in the US but all over the world. This is why the Bush administration was doing its level best to enlist the support of the movie industry as it embarked on a policy of war and aggression in the Middle East. It had been recently announced in the trades and on the mainstream news, for example, that the White House had approached various influential Hollywood executives to form an ad-hoc committee for the purpose of promoting American values in movies. Clearly, this was an attempt to introduce censorship through the back door, which if allowed to succeed would be the final nail in the coffin of the film industry as anything other than a propaganda ministry working on behalf of the dominant ideology.

Departing the rally, I walked all the way back to Connie's apartment, stopping off for a bite to eat and a short respite on the way. By the time I returned she'd left for work. I took the opportunity to get stuck into her wine collection.

14

Hollywood turns into a ghost town over the Christmas period. Comprised of a largely transient population, people leave LA in their thousands at this time of year to be with their families in other parts of the country or overseas. As a result of this mass albeit temporary migration, there is very little in the way of atmosphere to engender any Christmas spirit among those left behind. The lack of winter weather, of people walking the streets, all of it combines to turn Hollywood, and Los Angeles in general, into a dead zone during Christmas and New Year.

This year, staying put in LA, I was spending Christmas on my own. On the day itself I watched television for a few hours in the morning before, bored doing that, venturing out. I got into my car and drove around for an hour or two, heading downtown along and through eerily deserted streets. Then I took in a movie, before heading home via the Thai food place on Beverly Boulevard that I liked.

It was the best Christmas I ever had.

New Year's Eve found me working at a party on Rodeo Drive. I'd only taken the job thinking it would be the perfect way to mix and mingle while getting paid for the pleasure. But halfway through proceedings the fire marshall arrived and closed the party down, thus ending everybody's night on a sour note. Rodeo Drive in Beverly Hills was not a place to hold a party without a permit.

A few months later I had reason to return to Rodeo Drive, this world famous shopping thoroughfare synonymous with obscene wealth and consumerism. I was there during the day this time, when the place is alive with women sporting more plastic on their faces than flesh and bone, tired Hollywood players whose best days are behind them, not forgetting frenetic groups of mainly Japanese tourists. I had with me a bunch of antiwar leaflets and stickers, which I proceeded to spread around the disgracefully expensive shops, if only to briefly intrude on the bubble of vulgarity which this part of the world describes.

Come January, when the film and television industry opened up again, I found myself booked as a stand-in on a cop show called *Dragnet*, inspired by the show of the same name that was a veritable American cultural institution back in the fifties. The new version was in its first season and was shot at Universal Studios in North Hollywood, which was only a mere hop, skip, and a jump from my apartment.

The stand-in's role on any production, TV or movie, is to essentially take the place of one of the principle actor during the process of setting up a given shot. As such the role is critical to the ability of the crew to light the scene, set up the camera - or cameras in the case of a sitcom - and give the director an idea of how the scene's going to look when its shot with the principals. It is a role that requires you to look similar in size and appearance to the actor you are standing-in for. Even more important, it is vital that you are always on time and that you pay attention to everything that's going on. You need to study the initial scene rehearsal with the principals so you can replicate the choreography of the scene for the benefit of the director and director of photography (DP) before they shoot it for real. The importance of the role is reflected in the problems which ensue when performed badly.

One afternoon, I received a message from Central Casting requesting that I attend an interview to stand-in on an upcoming movie. The message left me underwhelmed. Attending an interview meant losing a day's pay. With no guarantee of work involved, it was a bad deal all round. Subsequently, I was less than happy.

The next day, with absolutely no idea what movie or which actor I was being considered to stand-in for, I made my way down to the production office in Culver City where the interviews were being held. I'd been asked to bring a resumé, but I didn't have a resumé for stand-in work and since I couldn't be bothered making one up, I arrived without one. Too bad, I thought to myself. If they want me for the role then they'll just have to take me as I am.

It was street parking outside the offices where the interviews were taking place and it took me a good twenty minutes to find a space. Entering the building, harassed and pissed off at the stress involved just getting here, I was directed upstairs to a waiting room, where I joined the half-dozen or so other guys being interviewed for the same gig. I recognized a couple of them from previous movies and TV shows I'd worked on in the past. We exchanged perfunctory nods as I took a seat to wait for my name to be called. Same old shit, I remember thinking. Nothing but a waste of time.

After a few minutes it felt uncomfortable us all sitting in such close proximity without speaking to one another. The realization that we were competing for the same role meant that surreptitiously, or as surreptitiously as possible, there was a lot of sizing up going on. By now I was sure that I had little or no chance of getting this gig; the others I'd noticed had brought resumes and pictures with them and they appeared serious and focused. Little wonder when you consider that stand-in gigs were much sought after in Hollywood. For extras it was considered the next step on the way to becoming a principal actor and then stardom. The fact that this was more myth than reality was neither here nor there. It was the commonly-held belief and therefore considered sacrosanct.

Finally, after around half an hour, it was my turn to be interviewed.

I followed the assistant along a corridor, embarrassed to be doing so without the requisite resumé and pictures in hand. I envisaged being abruptly dealt with and given what they call short shrift as a consequence. I was led into an office, where another woman was seated behind a desk. She got up, shook me by the hand, and introduced herself as Marci.

'Did you bring your resume?'

'Eh, no ... sorry. It needs updated and I didn't have time. I can email it over to you later though.'

She looked at me. It was make or break time. 'Okay,' she said finally. 'Make sure you do. I need to see that.'

'I understand. I'll update it and send it over as soon as I get home.'

'Who have you stood in for?'

I reeled off a few names, comprising a series of obscure TV actors and day players. Hardly big time.

'You ever stood in for an entire movie?'

I had to confess I hadn't. Again, I felt sure my chances of landing this gig were zero, so what was the point in lying? Marci then led me out into the corridor to measure my height and take a couple of polaroids. This completed, she once again emphasized the need to see my resumé. I assured her once again that I would email it to her later, and on that note we parted company.

By the time I got back to Hollywood, barely beating the rush-hour traffic and another hour onto the journey, Central had called and left a message telling me I'd been hired. They also revealed in the message that the actor I was going to be standing in for was Ben Affleck on his next movie *Surviving Christmas*, which as the title suggested was a Christmas movie - a Christmas comedy to be exact.

It was Thursday and my first day working on the movie was set for that coming Monday, only giving me three days to prepare. I told Kenny, a struggling filmmaker who lived in the same apartment block. He thought it was a fantastic opportunity - though I wasn't sure if he was just saying that to make me feel better. I wasn't looking forward to the responsibility involved. For the next ten weeks I couldn't afford to be anything other than professional, on-time and diligent. This would be unlike anything I'd done before, standing-in for the star of a big-budget movie for the entire length of the production. It seemed a daunting prospect.

While compared to most of the other members of the crew on the movie my fee would be small, with the overtime involved I'd still be walking out with a far heftier pay cheque than I was used to. With this money I anticipated getting some badly-needed maintenance done on the car, paying off a few bills, and still having some left over. Politics would have to take second place for a while. But that was okay. By telling myself that it was only for a comparatively short period of time, and that I needed the money, I found I was able to come to terms with the sacrifice involved.

Monday arrived and, unable to sleep, I was up at five. My call time was seven and crew parking was at a parking lot in Culver City, a twenty-minute drive depending on traffic. This meant I had some time to kill. I spent it eating a leisurely breakfast, watching the TV news, checking my emails, all the while experiencing dread like a large brick in the pit of my stomach.

Unable to stand hanging around the apartment any longer waiting for the time to pass, I showered, dressed and headed out. The sun was just coming up and the air was fresh and clean as I strolled down Sycamore Avenue. Passing Chuck, the security guard on duty outside the Scientology building on the corner of Hollywood Boulevard, I hit him with a smile. He was all right Chuck, at least for a Scientologist, and yet again I marvelled at the stamina involved in standing outside the same building for 12 hours a day every day with a smile on your face. Maybe there was something in this Scientology guff after all?

I crossed the boulevard, continued on down for half a block, and turned into the alley on my way to the parking garage where I paid sixty bucks a month to park the Chevy. Ramone was on duty at the garage this morning. He was a young Mexican kid working his way through college, struggling to survive along with the majority living in the land of the free.

I took Fountain Avenue to La Cienega, then La Cienega all the way to Culver City and crew parking. Judging by the few vehicles that were there when I turned in, I was one of the first to arrive. I parked, turned off the engine, grabbed my stuff and walked to one of three shuttle vans waiting to ferry the crew over to the set. This morning I had the luxury of a van to myself and I used the ten-minute journey to mentally prepare myself for what I knew was going to be a very busy and very long day.

Arriving at the soundstage, I was hit by the same scene of mayhem and organized chaos you find on every movie set. Everything seems out of sync when in actual fact it's all moving to a finely tuned rhythm and purpose. As there was still over half and hour to go before my official call time, my first port of call was the catering truck for some coffee and breakfast.

A few crew members were eating at the tables set up just inside the soundstage. I took my food and coffee and sat at the far end, content to be alone with my thoughts. A few minutes later I was interrupted by Marci arriving and handing me my voucher, before instructing me to report to wardrobe to be 'colour-coded' as soon as I was ready. Colour-coded means being fitted in an outfit that resembles in colour and style the outfit that the actor you're standing in for is going to be wearing on-camera. This allows the DP and the director to get an idea of how the shot will look with the actors in it, giving them the opportunity to make any adjustments that may be required.

I located the wardrobe trailer and upon presenting myself was handed a set of blue-striped pyjamas to put on. Dignity and self-respect, I realized, were words that I was going to have to banish from my vocabulary on this particular gig. I slipped the top and bottoms on over my clothes and trudged back to the stage to find and check in with Marci, conscious of being laughed at by the crew every step of the way. I couldn't see them laughing, nor could I hear them, but that didn't matter - it was enough that I could feel them.

Today's scenes were bedroom scenes, hence the pyjamas, and judging by the order of the scenes being shot that day, Affleck's character was involved in both.

In movies no more than two or three scenes are shot in any one day, while in television it's usually around seven or eight. This is because when it comes to making a movie the emphasis is on quality, whereas with television it's quantity.

Having said that, often it was hard to tell the difference.

Amid all the activity produced by the crew setting up the lights etc. I noticed Marci standing talking to a guy whom I presumed to be the First AD (assistant director). She saw me and beckoned me over. Like an obedient dog I went, painfully self-conscious of my ridiculous attire in the process. Marci introduced me to Ian, who as I'd rightly guessed was the First AD. He seemed very personable and friendly, hitting me with the usual chat about my accent and being from Scotland; the same chat I'd heard a thousand times since coming to LA and would hear a thousand times more. Ian looked to be somewhere in his mid- to late-forties. He possessed the weary countenance and spiritless gaze of someone who'd seen too many early mornings and late nights on movie sets all over the world, a man whose life had comprised work and little else. Getting to know him better, I was to learn that he intended to retire after this particular production wrapped. Little did he know that as well as being the last production he worked on, it would also be the worst.

After a minute or so of small talk, Marci instructed me to hang tight and wait to be called to the set to work on setting up the first shot of the day. The crew was still working away in the background, with the combined noise of hammers and drills, men climbing up and down ladders and voices barking out instructions jarring the senses. I did the only thing I could at this point and skulked off to find a chair and settle down with one of the two books I'd brought to keep me occupied during the anticipated long hours of inactivity.

I am now going to try and paint a picture of what it feels like sitting on an uncomfortable plastic chair in the middle of a soundstage reading a book dressed in a pair of blue-striped pyjamas on your first day standing-in for a Hollywood movie star. Intimidating comes close to describing it, as does humiliating, as does unnerving, as does embarrassing.

It's hard to fathom where such feelings of negativity stemmed from. The vast majority of guys I'd worked with as an extra would have been over the moon to be in my shoes right now. That I wasn't excited I think was a result of my conception of Hollywood as a town and an industry where a rigid caste system prevailed, with your intrinsice worth as a human being measured by your position on it. As an extra, first non-union and then union, I was used to being at the bottom of this totem pole. But working as an extra you never, or at least very rarely, come into direct contact with anyone higher up than a First AD; and even then only on occasion. Your contact is by and large with other extras, productions assistants and Second ADs.

However, as a stand-in, which in money and status ranks just a couple of notches higher than an extra (say just above that of a production assistant), you come into close contact and proximity to the director, principal actors, and even the producer or producers on occasion. What this does is accentuate your lowly status by comparison, magnifying it to the point where every time you walk onto the set to take your mark or go through a second team rehearsal, being pulled and pushed into position by the director or director of photography, the humiliation burns inside.

And yet despite this you'll run into a lot of stand-ins in Hollywood who are clearly labouring under the misconception that their shit doesn't stink, and who do their utmost to distance themselves from the extras for fear of being placed in the same bracket.

Surviving Christmas had been in production for a couple of weeks by the time I came onboard. It had spent that time shooting on location in Chicago, where the story was set, covering most of the exterior shots. They had used local people to stand-in for the actors in Chicago and according to Marci they'd proved useless. She'd gone out of her way to emphasise this point I could tell in an effort to get me fired up and focused. She didn't succeed.

About ten minutes or so after I sat down with my book, the call rang out: 'Second team! Drew second team!'

Drew was the name of Ben Affleck's character. They were calling me to set. It was time.

I got up, placed the book on top of the chair, and took my first tentative steps towards the set, which was located on a raised platform and necessitated climbing a set of wooden stairs. The grips, the hair and makeup girls, the set dressers, the electricians and cameramen, were all crowded into this small space, this mock-up of a typical adolescent's bedroom in Middle America. I was conscious of being studied and scrutinized. It was a surreal feeling, the eyes of so many boring into you at the same time, yet strangely it failed to throw me off. My self-consciousness had suddenly been replaced by adrenaline, producing a surge of confidence that manifested in a swagger in my step as I walked onto the set and announced to the DP in a commanding tone of voice:

'Where do you want me?'

'Lie down on the bed please.'

This I did, remaining there while the DP, whose name was Charlie, directed the cameras and lights with a series of instructions delivered in the manner of a sergeant-major addressing a company of raw recruits: short, sharp and aggressive.

After around half an hour the command 'Ready for first team' was given by Ian, the AD, before he approached me. 'You okay?' he asked. I nodded. 'Okay, thank you,' he said. 'We're ready for first team now.'

My role was over on this particular shot and I began making my way from the set. It was now that Ben Affleck appeared, wearing the exact same pyjamas as me, breezily greeting the crew in the manner of the movie star he was. Not once did he look in my direction, I noticed, though I could tell he was aware of my presence. As I departed the set, ducking under a couple of lights by the door on the way, I recalled my conversation with Marci after I'd been informed I'd been hired. She told me that Ben preferred to keep a professional distance from his stand-ins. I was not offended or put off in the slightest by this. Movie stars like Affleck needed to be careful when it came to who they allowed to get close. Their profile and fame made them prime targets for the paparazzi, who hunted them as a predator hunts its prey. Consequently, they needed to erect a firewall between themselves and the world beyond a trusted group of friends, family, and associates. This is just the way it was.

I returned to my plastic chair to find another guy sitting in close proximity. As I sat down he introduced himself as Steve, explaining that he was there to stand-in for the other principal actor who was in in the bedroom scene with Affleck. The name of the movie, as I said, was *Surviving Christmas*. It was a fluffy, feel-good comedy about a successful advertising executive in Chicago, played by Affleck, who upon finding himself alone as Christmas, and unhappy with life in general, comes up with the idea of returning to his childhood home, the scene of many happy Christmases growing up, to try and recapture those happy times. This he does by paying the typical blue-collar family that are now living in the house for the privilege of allowing him to spend Christmas with them.

Playing the part of the father of the family was James Gandolfini of *Sopranos* fame, one of the most powerful actors around. The mother was being played by Catherine O'Hara; the son, who Steve was standing-in for, by a young actor named Josh

Zuckerman, while Christina Applegate was playing the daughter. Her character becomes the love interest of the Ben Affleck character as the movie unfolds.

Steve and I quickly established common ground with a shared, cynical outlook on all things Hollywood. In fact if anything he was even more bitter and angry than I was, launching into a scathing attack on everyone and everything as we sat there bemoaning our fate. He soon began talking about the script he was writing - guaranteed, he claimed, to get picked up for a sizeable fee once it was completed to transform his life. I felt sorry for him. Like so many in this town, he was deluding himself, clinging on to the false hope of overnight success to help him cope with the harsh reality of life in Hollywood.

But then again who was I to puncture anyone's dreams? Maybe he would be one of the lucky few who do succeed. After all, a lucky few did sell scripts in this town for a lot of money. You read about them in the trade newspapers every other week - that so-and-so had just sold a spec script for $600,000 dollars to Disney about a boy who discovers he's really a cat with magical powers, for example. It was always funny to me how most of the big-selling spec scripts seemed to involve a ridiculous premise you would think would be laughed out of the room.

Anyway, returning to the movie, the first shot of the day took around an hour to complete. Afterwards, responding to the call, I made my way back to the set to work on preparing the next shot. I passed Affleck making his way out with his ever-present entourage in tow, heading for the luxury of his massive trailer parked just outside the soundstage. Reaching the set, I lay back down on top of the bed. This time, due to it being what they describe in the business as a two-shot, the other actor in the scene was included. This meant that my fellow stand-in Steve was also involved in the set-up. Watched by the director the two of us proceeded to go through the choreography of the scene, replicating the movements of the actors during their first-team rehearsal. The director's name was Mike, this was his breakthrough movie, and he was respectful and friendly to everyone. Ian the AD, as I've already said, seemed a good guy also, as did Jim the lighting gaffer. Marci was okay too - a bit uptight perhaps, but only due to the pressure of the role. In fact everyone on the crew worked under enormous pressure in an environment in which nothing was ever done fast enough, well enough, or efficiently enough to keep the producers satisfied. The result was a toxic atmosphere and the sense that you were only one mistake or misstep from being fired.

With this in mind, it was remarkable that anyone found it within themselves to smile or engage in friendly banter at all. That they did was a testament to the determination on the part of each of the aforementioned not to allow their humanity to be completely crushed under the wheels of the juggernaut that is Hollywood.

Charlie the DP was the only problem I had when it came to the crew. He wasn't just a bastard to me though, I'll give him that. He shouted and barked at everyone under him. His camera crew, the grips, the electricians, all of them got a dose. I was amazed that they took it. But then again this was Hollywood, a town and an industry where pride, self-respect and self-esteem are readily replaced by supplication and abasement in the interests of maintaining a career. Deciding it was time to get with the program, I verily applied myself to the task, seduced and swayed by the number of people I spoke to who assured me that I was so, so very fortunate to be standing-in for Ben Affleck.

Day after day I tumbled out of bed before the sun came up, determined not to be late, sometimes even squeezing in a run before eating a quick breakfast and jumping in the car for the drive down to Culver City. Running through Hollywood at five in the morning is an experience all by itself. In the dark, deserted, the streets take on a life of their own. I would typically run all the way along Hollywood Boulevard to Laurel Canyon, about a mile and half in distance, then down to Sunset, before heading back to La Brea, where I'd turn left and struggle back up to Hollywood and home again. It never failed to rejuvenate me, pick me up and get me set for the twelve hours of monotony to come.

While the bulk of the movie was being shot on the soundstage in Culver City, focusing on interior scenes, there were still a few exterior scenes to be shot, which due to lack of time had not been covered when the production had been on location in Chicago in the first couple of weeks of shooting. These exteriors were shot at various locations in and around LA County. The three days we spent in a surburban shithole of a small town by the name of Orange, roughly ninety minutes south of LA, stands out for all the wrong reasons. The drive there and back was torture on a gridlocked freeway. The scene being shot involved hundreds of extras, all dressed as if it was winter in Chicago. No expense or effort was spared in turning this small southern Californian town into a Chicago suburb in the depths of winter either; the production pumping in tons of fake snow, putting up loads of Christmas street decorations, doing and spending whatever it took achieve the authenticity required.

Every minute I was there was a minute of my life wasted.

Meanwhile, the build up of military forces in the Middle East was continuing apace. The noises coming from Bush and his cabinet - from the likes of Rumsfeld, Cheney, Powell and Rice - were alarming. It was obvious that the United Nations and international law were about to be discarded in the Bush administration's determination to invade Iraq. This was at at time when over 40 million Americans had no healthcare provision whatsoever; 30 million were officially below the poverty line, with 8 million of those children; 2 million were incarcerated in prison, seventy percent of them non-white, with an additional 5 million caught up in the judicial system in some shape or form.

Brutal is the only word to describe the level of social and economic injustice that held sway in every major city and town in the land of the free. In LA incidents of police brutality against blacks occurred on an almost weekly basis; and those just the ones that made the news.

My contact with the antiwar movement during this period consisted of regular phone calls to the office for updates, along with attending the odd meeting whenever my schedule allowed. The regular activists were always guaranteed to be around, but by now their presence in the office was bolstered by more and more who'd come into the movement as the build-up to war continued. The meetings were still packed and lively, and I never failed to come away from one filled with the sense of purpose that was absent from every other aspect of my life.

My efforts to establish a career as a screenwriter in Hollywood remained centred around the project that was in development with Jack and Tom at Pilot Films. Every other week or so I'd get an email informing me how things were progressing in their efforts to attract interest in the project. They were determined, I'll give them that much, but it was becoming increasingly obvious that for whatever reason the script was not capturing the imagination of the industry. At one point, Jack managed to get John MacKenzie interested in the script, a British director whose work I'd always admired. He directed the British gangster classic movie *The Long Good Friday*, in addition to *A Sense Of Freedom, Just A Boy's Game*, and *Just Another Saturday*, each depicting the harsh reality of life on the mean streets of Glasgow as no director has ever managed before or since. That each of the aforementioned classic films and TV dramas were made in the late seventies and early eighties made no difference. The fact that John MacKenzie was interested in directing a script I'd written was a source of immense pride and personal satisfaction.

But, alas, in the course of the conference calls we had, along with some of the notes he subsequently came up with suggesting various alterations and changes to the characters and the story, it was clear that agreeing a final draft was going to prove elusive.

In the end John was gracious enough to pull out. He'd enjoyed a long career and the last thing he needed was to be attached to a project that was yet to attract finance with a writer and producer he was unable to find common ground with when it came to the script.

As for Tom, he'd set up a few meetings for me with various production companies around town, first sending each of them my script, which they read and liked enough to take things to the stage of a general meeting. When attending these meetings you were expected to have a couple of ideas for other scripts to pitch, and when you pitched them you had to make them sound interesting, otherwise you wouldn't be in the room for long.

The first of these meetings I attended, I arrived completely unprepared with no fully-worked-out ideas for new material to offer and even less of a clue as to the protocol involved. The offices of this particular production company were located in Santa Monica. They were housed in an impressive art-deco building, and arriving early I sat outside in the car for fifteen minutes trying to think up an idea for a movie.

The interior of the building was every bit as impressive as the exterior, well-designed and expensively appointed, just as you'd expect a successful movie production company's office would be. It was Jan De Bont's company, fresh off producing the highly successful *Speed* movies starring Keanu Reeves. At the time De Bont had a first look deal with one of the big studios - meaning they paid him a retainer to ensure that they were given first refusal on any new projects or scripts he was developing. It was a common arrangement between the studios and various high profile actors, producers and directors in the industry.

I sat in reception flipping through a magazine for around ten minutes before a woman appeared and introduced herself. I can't remember her name now, but I'd guess she was roughly my age. She was friendly and smiley in that insincere way I'd become accustomed to in Hollywood as she showed me into a private office, where I sat down on a sofa against the wall. She sat in the armchair chair opposite, whereupon the bullshit commenced.

We spoke about the weather for a few minutes, the topic inevitably inducing her to ask about Scotland and the weather over there. Then she made a few positive comments about my script, saying how it was different from the stuff that usually landed on her desk (oh really?), and so on. Throughout I was replaying the pitch for the idea I'd come up with in the car earlier, nervous in case I made an arse of myself. It was about a guy who takes on a major bank on Wall Street after they push his father to suicide by foreclosing on his home in some small Midwest American town.

Finally, the moment arrived. She asked me what else I was working on and I launched into my pitch. She sat listening, her face set in stone. The first thing she wanted to know when I ended was what my motivation for telling this particular story was. I told her that my decision to tell this particular story was because most people don't trust Wall Street, viewing its giant banks and financial institutions as out-of-control monoliths run by an unaccountable elite responsible for ruining the lives of millions at home and throughout the developing world with their predatory lending and unethical investments.

She stared at me for a few moments, before informing me that her father was an executive on Wall Street. Furthermore, she went on, I was completely wrong in my assertions that most people were distrustful of banks or corporations in general. Most people saw them as wealth creators and employers, and as such indispensable to the US economy and American way of life. And all this stuff about ruining millions of lives, well that was just ludicrous, she asserted. The reason why the Third World was in such a shitty state wasn't down to the role of corporations. In fact, if it wasn't for those corporations investing and creating jobs in poor countries the people there would be in an even worse state.

My feet hit the sidewalk five minutes later.

15

By now I'd had enough working as Ben Affleck's stand-in. This was slightly ironic considering the production staff thought I was doing a great job. Where a stand-in is concerned doing a good job means being on time and ensuring that nobody ever has to come looking for you when you're needed on set. It means that when you're on set, you are able to repeat to a tee the action and movement of the actor that you are standing in for. Succeed and you pass muster. Fail and you hold up the shot in the one business in the world where time is most definitely money. Yet even though it was a regular gig and relatively well paid, enough was enough.

I broke the news to Marci early one morning in the parking garage adjacent to the location in downtown LA, where the movie was shooting that week. I caught her as she emerged from her car and I from mine as we arrived for work. Upon receiving the news she looked at me with a stunned expression on her face. Then she shook her head and said: 'No...you can't. You just can't.'

I was bewildered by her reaction. I knew that she and the rest of the production staff thought highly of me. But so what? I was merely a stand-in and as such eminently replaceable. At least that's how I saw it.

But not according to Marci. She went on to assure me that moves were afoot to correct 'the problem', as she referred to it; that she couldn't say too much right now but that rest assured by the end of the week 'the problem' would no longer exist. It was obvious that by 'the problem' she meant Charlie, who by this point was making everyone's life a misery on set. I certainly didn't get the worst of his shit, but nonetheless I was finding it harder to take.

As a result of this exchange I went through the entire day filled with mixed feelings. I knew that even if 'the problem' was resolved I still wanted to quit. I was sick of it - sick of having to be up at the crack of dawn every morning to work between twelve and fourteen hours a day as a stand-in five days a week; and sometimes six if the production fell behind schedule. I'd been doing the job for two months by now and I was tired. Moroever, being nothing more than another man's flunkey was playing havoc with my self-esteem. Day in day out Affleck would waltz on to the set surrounded by an entourage of hangers-on. The way they all laughed at his jokes and bent over backwards to keep him happy was stomach churning, as was the hoopla that took place whenever his then-girlfriend J-Lo arrived for a visit.

No, fuck it, I'd had enough.

We were now shooting scenes set in the mock-up of a luxury penthouse apartment. The production had taken over an old now defunct luxury hotel in downtown LA, recreating a luxury penthouse apartment in what used to be the ballroom. It never ceased to amaze me how much time, money and effort Hollywood put into recreating authenticity. Entering the set it truly felt as if you were in a luxury apartment in downtown Chicago at Christmas time. The scene painters had outdone themselves with their recreation of the Chicago skyline outside the fake windows. I had to look twice to make sure it wasn't the real thing.

The second team rehearsals we ran through over the three days of shooting here were particularly exhaustive and intense. They were scenes in which Affleck's character wanders listlessly around his apartment, lonely and depressed at the prospect of spending Christmas alone.

One of the producers came up to me one day in a break between set-ups, and apropos of my earlier conversation with Marci took me aside to assure me that by the end of that week I could look forward to everything being resolved. The cryptic manner of first Marci and now this producer, whose name I've since forgotten, was evocative of some Machiavellian plot being underway. You would have to have been an idiot not to understand that what they were telling me, without actually telling me, was that Charlie was about to be fired and replaced. If only they knew that by now it wasn't just him making my life on set a misery but the entire experience, they wouldn't have been so attentive and sensitive in their dealings with me. I wanted out and so instead of being happy and grateful at the news, I was crushed that my excuse for leaving was being pulled out from under my feet.

Unlike the last major antiwar demo held in San Francisco in October of 2002, which the LA branch had helped to build, it had been decided by the national leadership to hold a separate demonstration in LA on February 15, 2003, in addition to one in San Francisco a day later; this to capitalize on the huge groundswell of antiwar sentiment that was now prevalent across the country. More crucially, on this date coordinated marches and demonstrations were scheduled to take place all over the world in an international day of protest. We were confident that an LA demonstration would attract sufficient numbers to make it a worthwhile endeavour.

With the ante having been significantly upped by Bush and his administration, evident in the way that the military build up in the Middle East was gathering pace, I was growing increasingly frustrated at not being able to engage in as much political activity as I would have liked due to the constraints that came with working on the movie. The producers had kept to their word by firing Charlie and his camera and lighting crew. In his place arrived a new DP in the shape of Manny, along with his crew. The atmosphere on set was transformed as a result, positive and friendly where before it had been negative and hostile. Manny soon revealed himself a man in the mould of that long tradition of American liberalism exemplified by the likes of Franklin D Roosevelt, JFK, and Jimmy Carter. He was most definitely antiwar and anti-Bush, which, surrounded by a crew which consisted of a fair contingent of rednecks, patriots and right wing yee-ha Republicans, made for a welcome change.

In line with the gathering cloud of war a custom began on the set whereby people began to articulate their political views by writing them on the walls of the bathroom. It was located next to the soundstage and the walls were soon covered, people using the felt pens that were left lying there for that very purpose by whoever was behind the exercise. This proved salutary in that it enabled people to vent their views under cover of anonymity and without opening the door to confrontation with fellow crew members. In fact a policy had been introduced banning the discussion of politics on set. However, it proved impossible to enforce given the magnitude of what was taking place and the extent to which it was dominating the news.

I recall discussing the impending war with Affleck's personal bodyguard on a couple of occasions. His name was Scott. He was an ex-Marine who told me that he'd once served in Iraq as a guard at the former US Embassy in Baghdad. Big, raw and serious, unsurprisingly he supported Bush and was a keen adherent of the 'let's go in and kick some ass' school of international affairs. Day after day he followed Affleck onto the set, wherepon he would stand off to the side while Affleck was shooting his scene, before following him back out to his trailer once he'd finished. On one memorable occasion, while we were shooting airport scenes out at Air Hollywood, a specially designed soundstage located way out in the Valley replicating an airport and where they had a life-size mock up of the interior of a passenger aircraft, he began panicking when he lost sight of Affleck and couldn't find him. I'll never forget the sight of this tough ex-Marine running up and down asking everyone from the craft service guy to the wardrobe girls if they'd seen Ben. Hopefully, I remember thinking to myself at the time, this bodes well for the Iraqi people, who at that point were facing an invasion of their country by thousands just like him.

As for Ben Affleck, I'd grown to despise him. In fact it wasn't so much him (after all, I didn't know the man) but what he represented that I despised. Witnessing the power he had over so many people, watching them supplicate themselves in front of him and doing their utmost to ingratiate themselves, sickened me. Luckily, I was able to take comfort in the fact that February 15 was fast approaching. On that day millions across the entire world were set to come together to raise their voices as one against war. It was a good feeling to know that I was going to be part of it.

A typical day's shooting on the movie wrapped around seven in the evening. If we were shooting at the soundstage in Culver City, I could make it to the office across town in twenty minutes or so, depending on the traffic. The organizing meeting on any given evening would already have begun by the time I arrived, but due to the fact they were always passionate and vibrant affairs, with the office stowed out with people, they were well worth attending regardless.

Among the crew, apart from Manny, there were two or three other fellow travellers who began to make their feelings known. One of them, Lisa, worked in the props department. She was a feisty woman of Irish stock and whenever the subject of George Bush came up she would launch into a shower of invective the likes of which her ancestors would have been proud. I gave her a leaflet advertising the upcoming demo and she assured me she'd be there with some of her friends and neighbours.

Alan was one of the assistant cameramen who'd arrived to work on the movie as part of Manny's crew. He was in his late-forties, diminutive in stature, quietly spoken and just about the last guy you might expect to hold radical political views. Yet radical they were. At college in the late seventies he'd been in a group that was modelled on the old SDS (Students for a Democratic Society), which had played a pivotal role in the US

Civil Rights and antiwar movements of the sixties. He spoke of those days with a sparkle in his eye, waxing lyrical about the likes of Tom Hayden, Malcolm X, and a whole raft of other sixties radicals. He had been inactive politically more or less since leaving college and starting work (a career in Hollywood hardly leaves you with enough time to eat and shit never mind engage in politics), but with Bush and all that was going on in the Middle East he was angry again, he told me.

So, yes, there were a few among the crew who were against the war.

But there's a difference between being against something and being willing to do something about it. It was hard for me now to understand apathy and inactivity in people. Yet for years, before becoming active myself, this had been me, holding views but unwilling to vocalize them at a protest or join with a group to work towards having those views heard. Back then I used to regard people who stood in the street handing out leaflets and went on protest marches as a different breed. They dressed, spoke and behaved in a way that was alien to me, and as a result I could never identify with them. What I later came to understand was that being an activist is not about how you dress, speak or behave per se. It should never be viewed as a lifestyle choice, which by definition sets you apart from mainstream society, from the very people with whom you should be trying to connect. You don't recruit or attract people by being unlike them, even though many within the movement had clearly fallen into this trap. All you do when you go down this path is alienate most people before you get a chance to share your views with them. It's the difference between an outward looking approach to politics and an inward looking one. For me the former was much more relevant than the latter.

By the time February 15 came round the buzz in and around LA was palpable. Teams of activists had ensured that posters advertising the demo were stuck up all over the city; others were manning stalls outside supermarkets, shopping malls, sports events, and every other event or place you could think of where people gathered in large numbers. Over a hundred activists were working flat out round the clock to build the demo in the days and weeks leading up to it, and the volume of calls into the office on any given day was immense. Though still working twelve-hour days on the movie, I had personally stuck hundreds of leaflets on the windscreens of hundreds of cars parked in and around Hollywood, doing so early in the morning before heading to work.

The route of the march was basically the entire length of Hollywood Boulevard, from east to west, then down a couple of blocks to the Orange and La Brea intersection for the closing rally. This meant that I could walk to the demo from my apartment on Sycamore.

Of course, people could march and protest all they wanted. The question was: would those in power pay any heed?

The answer was obvious to me even before the question was asked. It was an unequivocal and resounding no. To believe anything else was the product of idealism, wishful thinking, and/or a lack of understanding of history - perhaps all three combined. When it came to the world's only superpower, a nation founded on the genocide of the indigenous people of the north American continent, a nation in which the institution of human slavery was enshrined in its founding documents, its path had always been one of war and conquest. In truth it would be difficult to find going back as far as ancient times a more inhumane and violent power as the United States and the empire it had forged. Yet throughout its history of wars, barbarism and the subversion of human rights around the world, the US had succeeded in propagating the lie that words such as freedom and democracy were the motor force of its existence. It was a lie begun by the Founding Fathers in order to motivate their fellow countrymen to fight and die in a revolution whose objective, rather than forge a nation in which all men are created equal, was to wrench political and economic power away from a British monarch and transfer it to themselves - fifty-five rich white men the majority of whom were slave owners. The Bush administration had set its entire machine on unleashing war on Iraq, with 9/11 the pretext it needed to carry out what was a pre-9/11 agenda of cementing US hegemony in the oil-rich Middle East and beyond.

Before leaving for the demo, I checked the news. I was keen to get reports on the demonstrations around the world that had already begun or taken place given the time difference. The news was staggering. Two million were estimated to have marched in London; three million in Rome; another million or two in Florence; hundreds of thousands in Paris; a million and a half in Madrid.

A more emphatic message of dissent could not have been sent to both the Bush administration in Washington and the Blair government in London. Speaking of which, the report that grabbed me most was of the the two million who'd marched through the British capital. It was the largest demonstration ever seen in Britain, the report stated, and gleefully I thought about how devastated Bush's poodle, Tony Blair, must now be feeling.

Making my way to the assembly point for the LA march and demonstration, I even began to entertain the possibility that we might, just might, succeed in stopping the impending war after all, completely reversing the cold logic of my previous position.

What was it Gramsci had said again: *'Pessimism of the intellect. Optimism of the will'.*

By now reports were emerging of a schism within the Bush administration over Iraq. Colin Powell was not it was rumoured as hellbent on war as others within the government. Unlike his colleagues it appeared he was mindful of international law and the need to acquire at least the patina of legitimacy before going ahead. This provided us with hope, especially considering that within the UN Security Council Russia, France and Germany were against going to war on Iraq and would not give the US the UN mandate they required to provide the legal cover to start one. Perhaps the sight of millions protesting around the world on the same day might succeed in proving the catalyst for a political crisis.

Meanwhile, Hans Blix and his team of weapons inspectors were scouring every corner of Iraq searching for WMD that did not exist. Most people with eyes to see and ears to listen with already suspected as much. Even people like Scott Ritter, former weapons inspector, ex-US Marine and confirmed Republican, had come out and said so. Iraq's nuclear, biological and chemical weapons programs had either been destroyed in the first Gulf War back in 1991, dismantled by Ritter and his colleagues in the aftermath, or simply could no longer have been sustained under an ensuing thirteen year UN sanctions regime that had more than succeeded in destroying the country's infrastructure. Then too was the fact, the incontrovertible fact, that above all else Saddam was a survivor; despite a deluge of propaganda to the contrary, he was no madman with a doomsday scenario for the Middle East in mind. He was not a jihadist with dreams of paradise in an afterlife, nor was he blind to the fact that any kind of challenge to the US would be akin to suicide, both for him and his people.

He may have been many things, but crazy wasn't one of them. If any world leader was crazy it was George W. Bush, a man who believed he enjoyed a direct line to God and had surrounded himself with an assortment of swivel-eyed, rapture-ready Christian fundamentalists.

Halfway along Hollywood Boulevard on my way to the corner of Hollywood and Vine, it struck me how this decaying and rundown street of broken dreams was once the centre of the entertainment business, where legends of the silver screen used to congregate and be seen frequenting the fancy restaurants and nightclubs that once predominated here. I tried hard to imagine the likes of Clark Gable, Errol Flynn, Bette Davis, Joan Crawford and the other stars of Hollywood's golden age being ferried to places like the Brown Derby for dinner or to the Roosevelt Hotel, where the first Oscar award ceremonies were held way back when. In their place now was a succession of cheap and tacky souvenir stores, tattoo parlors, and fast food restaurants.

To see the expressions of deep disappointment and shock on the faces of the busloads of tourists visiting the Chinese Mann Theater, protected and corralled by private security guards while they scurried around taking pictures, was something to behold. No doubt about it: Hollywood as the centre of the entertainment industry was well and truly over: Hollywood as a pit of effluvium and decay had arrived.

Three blocks from Vine the sidewalks were full of protesters. They wore T-shirts with slogans like 'No War' and 'Don't Bomb Iraq'. Many carried flags and banners with slogans like 'Bombing For Peace Is Like Fucking For Virginity' and 'Regime Change Starts At Home.'

The time was 11.30, the march was set to begin at noon, and people were pouring into the intersection, arriving in cars, buses, and emerging from the underground station in one neverending stream. The usual multitude of stalls had been set up selling the usual array of T-shirts, hats, scarves, flags, books and magazines. All of them were packed with people milling aroud. The sound truck was parked around the corner, with various people working on it making last minute adjustments to the microphone and speakers. As arranged, I made my way over to the ANSWER stall, where others were already congregated. They too had heard reports of the huge demos that had taken place in other cities around the world and as a result the excitement and anticipation was palpable. Everyone was eager to get started.

The sound truck was manoeuvred so that it faced the route of the march - east along Hollywood Boulevard. The first of the opening rally speakers took to the mic and the crowd began to cheer. And still they came, more and more people arriving. The numbers were beyond our best expectations and predictions. Ivor and Mandy were up on the truck marshalling the speakers, while the rest of us put on our bibs and took up position as stewards at the front.

Finally, the speeches came to an end and the march was ready to start. The noise, the banners and flags, the tens of thousands of people packed in behind the sound truck that was about to lead the way, all of it was incredible. Hank was driving the sound truck, while Ivor was on the back leading the chants on the mic. Thousands of voices joined in, ensuring that the truck edged forward accompanied by a wall of noise.

I have so many memories of that day that it's hard to separate them into any kind of order. Marching proudly along Hollywood Boulevard for about a mile we looked tremendous, 70,000 people with our myriad banners and flags, mesmerizing onlookers and pedestrians who'd been subjected to a barrage of pro-war propaganda on the news day and night since 9/11. We were the antiwar movement, we were serious, and we were big and growing bigger. This was the statement we were making not only here in Hollywood but all over the world. Marching alongside so many who at that moment had transcended their own narrow self interests in a society in which individualism held sway was a proud moment. This was about the power of the collective, and what power. That intangible-yet-palpable bond of solidarity when thousands of people come together as one was more powerful than I ever could have imagined.

The closing rally as ever was by turns brilliant, not so brilliant, mediocre and downright boring. To my mind the movement always tried to squeeze in too many speakers at mass demonstrations. Politically, there was little choice, given that each of the organizations involved in setting up these events did so on the understanding that they would be allowed the same number of speakers to represent them and their point of view. Regardless, for the people there it got tedious after an hour or so and invariably many melted away. However, the most important thing was the march. It had been tremendous; not as massive as the previous mass demonstration in San

Francisco, but excellent nonetheless. What gave it an added dimension was the fact it had been held as part of an international day of protest which the very next day prompted the *New York Times* to describe the global antiwar movement as the new superpower.

By the time the final speaker left the stage there was hardly anybody left apart from activists, stewards, and a few diehards. All of us were in high spirits, delighted with the massive turnout and unforgettable atmosphere.

The LAPD had been out in force while remaining conspicuous by the subtle distance they'd kept throughout the day. In fact they'd been extremely cooperative, communicating and negotiating with us respectfully and anxious to ensure that the march passed off smoothly without any undue interference. This was in sharp contrast to the first demonstration I attended in LA back in 2000 at the Democratic National Convention, when the police had steamed into the crowd with tear gas and what can only be described as a full blown cavalry charge. Make no mistake, the LAPD, renowned for being aggressive in their dealings with the public, especially ethnic minorities and the working class, had not suddenly undergone a cultural epiphany since then; they had not suddenly adopted a more sensitive or conciliatory outlook and approach to policing. What had changed was the size of the crowd they were dealing with. It was this and this alone that had determined the change in their approach.

16

The Monday after the demonstration saw me arrive for the start of another week on the movie in high spirits. The enormous size and number of demonstrations that had taken place around the world had hit the headlines, managing to knock the pro-war consensus within the mainstream off the front pages of all the major newspapers, as well as relegating them in order of importance on the TV news bulletins.

On the set it was interesting to hear the differing opinions of the antiwar movement. More than a few, consisting of those who supported Bush without equivocation or condition and wholeheartedly believed in the 'mission' to get Saddam, dismissed the protesters as traitors. Others, more liberal in outlook, though still of the belief that the US was the greatest nation on earth, abhorred the Bush administration. Conscious of what they referred to as 'America's place in the world', which they viewed as a shining example for other nations to follow rather than a hammer to be feared and loathed, they watched aghast as Bush and his cronies set about turning their beloved country into a rogue state. The liberal antiwar stance they espoused was reflective of the view that the US should only go to war against Iraq under a UN mandate and not unilaterally. They weren't concerned about the damage that had already been done to the Iraqi people by over a decade of crippling sanctions, nor were they overly concerned at the prospect of innocent Iraqis being blown to smithereens if the US went ahead and attacked. Their primary concern was the welfare of the troops (our boys) and America's image and standing in the eyes of the world. In other words, they supported the same aims as the neocons - namely US hegemony and domination - but advocated different, subtler means of achieving those aims. This difference in form not content is what separated Democrats and Republicans and had done more or less throughout the nation's history.

The first shot of the day on the movie involved the entire cast sitting around the kitchen table in a breakfast scene. It was good to be able to sit through a set-up for once. It was also a welcome change to be working on a scene with the other stand-ins, rather than by myself which was usually the case. The atmosphere on set had been transformed, as mentioned earlier, by the change in the DP. Now people were actually nice to one another and there was none of the tension and ill feeling that predominated previously.

Even so, I was finding it increasingly difficult to keep up the pretence.

By now word had gotten round that I was involved in the antiwar movement, and I began to detect hostility from various quarters as a consequence. Affleck's bodyguard Scott for example had taken to throwing me dirty looks when he wasn't ignoring me completely. The same with his personal assistant. Too bad.

There remained one or two sympathetic voices on the crew as well, though. Sadly they weren't very vocal, preferring to keep their antiwar and anti-Bush sentiments quiet. Their reluctance to speak out was illustrative of the fear, now commonplace, of being labelled unpatriotic or anti-American. It was a fear prevalent not just on the set of this movie but within the country as a whole.

Later that day another UN debate was due to be held on Iraq, on whether or not the Iraqi government was complying with the inspections that were now scouring the country looking for stockpiles of WMD. Despite being at work, I was determined to listen to some of the proceedings on the radio one way or the other, especially now that events were approaching the point of no return.

Finally, Manny announced that the shot was ready and the call went up for first team. Along with my fellow stand-ins, I began making my way off the set to make way for the principals, who began to arrive in their usual ones and twos. James Gandolfini as ever was the first to appear, hitting everyone with his customary jovial smile and friendly greeting as he took up his position, shaking hands with me as we passed one another. I was just heading over to the corner of the soundstage where the stand-ins were congregated when the soundstage door opened and in came Affleck's entourage, followed by the man himself. Standing directly in their path it was a moment that called for acknowledgment in the form of a nod or a polite greeting. But this was Hollywood, where a different kind of normality prevailed, and all five of them walked right past me as if I didn't exist, had never existed, and would never exist in any shape or form worthy of recognition. I continued on over to my chair and picked up the book I was reading - the *Communist Manifesto* by Karl Marx and Frederich Engels - and resumed reading where I'd left off.

> *'The history of all hitherto existing society is the history of class struggles. Freemen and slave, patrician and plebian, lord and serf, guild-master and journeyman, in a word, oppressor and oppressed, stood in constant opposition to one another, carried on an uninterrupted, now hidden, now open fight, a fight that each time ended, either in a revolutionary reconstitution of society at large, or in the common ruin of the contending classes.'*

Five or ten minutes later, I got up again and began walking across the soundstage in the direction of the exit, heading for the bathroom. As I passed the set I could hear the voices of Ben Affleck and his many sycophants, interspersed with loud laughter. Suddenly, Affleck led off on a rendition of the US national anthem, the *Star-Spangled Banner*. Almost immediately he was joined by others, until the entire set was united in song.

I continued on my way to the bathroom. What else could I do? I was desperate for a shit.

17

On March 18 2003 President George W. Bush informed the American people and the world at large that he had ordered Saddam Hussein, his sons, and leading members of his regime to leave Iraq within the next 24 hours.

Along with various other members of the crew, I watched his broadcast to the nation in the set-medic's office, located in a normally quiet corner of the soundstage. No one uttered a word throughout, though the tension was thick. Lisa, the woman from the props department who'd marched against the war on Februrary 15, was in tears, and it was all I could do to stop myself joining her. Even the pro-war members of the crew were subdued as they watched the president. I remember thinking to mysef that the world would never be the same.

Thankfully I had to return to work, otherwise I would only have grown more and more depressed watching Bush spout his usual bellicose shite. However, like everybody else, I found it near impossible to remain focused. Suddenly nothing seemed to matter, and certainly not a meaningless Hollywood movie. As soon as I could I called the ANSWER office. As expected, they were busy making preparations for the emergency demo that had been planned in advance to take place on the evening of the first day of hostilities. The war was imminent, probably within a day or so, and driving home that night I felt numb, my head filled with thoughts of the countless people about to lose their lives, about a nation that was about to come under attack from the most destructive and powerful military the world had ever known.

It was late afternoon the very next day, March 19, when the world spread among the crew that airstrikes had started over Baghdad. My heart sank as soon as I heard the news. The only thing left for me to consider now was what to do in response.

Should I walk off the movie in protest; should I say something first and then walk off. Or should I remain and carry on working, in the realization that either way nothing would change. By this point there were only two weeks of shooting left before the production wrapped. That coming weekend the shoot was scheduled to move up to Big Bear, a popular ski resort north of LA. My hotel room and space on the bus had already been booked. Apart from Iraq this was the only thing the crew were talking about, with everybody anticipating three days of partying and fun in the snow. By this point too I had been approached by Affleck's people to work on his next movie, a John Woo action movie called *Paycheck*, which was scheduled to commence shooting up in Canada more or less immediately after this one wrapped.

Part of me was attracted by the offer of further employment, viewing it as an opportunity to finally achieve a semblance of financial security. I was aware that in a town where out of army of people who arrive hoping to find work, most find themselves locked into a perennial struggle to make ends meet, I was one of the fortunate ones. After all, who knows where this could lead, what other opportunities it might open up? Guys like De Niro and Hoffman had kept the same stand-ins for years and had them on lucrative contracts. They took them all over the world with them, and even gave them bit-parts in their movies from time to time.

But as strong as the voice urging me to accept the opportunity was, pointing out all the pluses involved, another even stronger voice was arguing the opposite. So what? You're just another man's flunkey. This is not what you uprooted and moved all the way out here for. Fuck the money. It can't be about that. Better working in the shittiest bar or nightclub, better struggling by on minimum wage, than being a movie star's underling.

But any internal wrangling over whether or not I should take up the offer was immediately set aside as soon as the bombs and the missiles started falling on Iraq. Though I'd expected and anticipated it would come to this, it was a shock when it arrived nonetheless. In a flash the job became surplus to requirements, and it was all I could do to stay until that day's shooting wrapped. As soon as it did I was out of there on the double quick, heading across town to the ANSWER office on Western Avenue in East LA.

I arrived to be met by a scene of bedlam: phones going, people busy typing on computers, others arriving and leaving in one never-ending stream. The TV news was on in the far corner. Along with Peter, Frank and others I stood watching it completely transfixed. Footage of bombs and missiles exploding all over Baghdad were being transmitted, accompanied by a solemn though dispassionate commentary. Nobody uttered a word. In the year 2003 a brutal imperialist war of aggression was being unleashed on a near defenceless people. It was a sickening spectacle.

After half an hour or so it was time to get to work helping organize and spread the word about the impromptu emergency demo that had been planned to take place the very next evening at five outside the Federal Building on Wilshire Boulevard. We hadn't sought or received a permit to hold the demo, which meant there was a strong possibility of confrontation with the police. Even as I was on the phone exhorting people to come out, I was unsure if I would be there myself. Work on the movie meant I wouldn't be able to get there until well after seven, by which time it would probably be over. What to do? I was scheduled to work, there was no one who could fill in, and even if there was the producers wouldn't allow it.

In the end the decision was made for me. I had almost forgotten how good it was to be among people who shared the same worldview and ideology, the same passion for radical politics. These were my comrades and the office was home. Nothing else came close.

We worked through to midnight building the demonstration. Afterwards we congregated in the 24-hour diner just along the street, scene of many a social gathering after meetings. Replacing shock over the start of the war by this point was anger. Peter in particular was more animated than I'd ever seen him, banging the table with his fist as he drove home this or that point. Around the table there was no hesitation or equivocation when it came to where our loyalties lay. They were squarely with the Iraqi people. Peter had visited Iraq some years before and witnessed first hand the devastation wrought by the sanctions. He was convinced that the majority of Iraqis would resist any occupation, regardless of their feelings about Saddam. He reminded us of Iraq's history of resistance to colonialism, of how the British and their puppet Iraqi regime was deposed in 1958, of how the Iraqis were a fiercely proud and independent people with a strong sense of national identity. It was a barnstorming performance.

It was around six-thirty the following morning that I picked up the phone and dialled Marci's number. The call went straight to her voicemail.

'Marci, I've decided to quit. There's a protest taking place against the war this afternoon and I need to be there. I'm sorry but this is too important. Take care. Bye.'

I never heard from Marci or anyone else from the movie again. Months later I ran into Robert, who'd stood in for James Gandolfini on the movie. We were both working on a *Toys R Us* commercial. He told me that the production staff were pissed off with me for quitting without notice and that they'd had to scramble around over the next couple of days to find a replacement.

I felt slightly guilty when Robert told me this. Marci and various others on the crew had been kind to me and letting them down had not been my intention. What I had done had been unprofessional to say the least. However, such sentiments paled in comparison with bombs and missiles being rained down on a civilian population. They did for me at least.

As predicted, the demo developed into a stand off with the LAPD. It had been scheduled to start at five, and I got there half an hour before to help set up banners, stalls, and the portable sound system we were usuing. The police were out in force. Three police choppers were circling overhead, I counted four LAPD armoured cars parked on the street, and there was phalanx of cops in riot gear lined up in front of us. Meanwhile, on our side, only around five or six hundred people had shown up, a far cry from the thousands who'd attended the last demo in Hollywood. Little did we realize that the start of hostilities in Iraq would spell the end of the mass movement as we knew it; the Bush administration cynically equating protesting the war with undermining the troops in harm's way. After all, so the propaganda went, 'our boys' are over there fighting to spread democracy and protect the American people from the threat of more 9/11s.

The cops did not intend to let us march. They had cordoned off a large section of Wilshire Boulevard, stopping the traffic in both directions, and had us boxed in. Using the portable sound system, we organized a small platform of speakers to address the crowd. Among some of the younger protesters there was a desire for militancy and confrontation. This would have been madness under the circumstances. At a certain point a mass sit-down was staged across the entire width of the road. After about half an hour the police began to move in, at the same time ordering everyone to disperse via loudspeaker. As they came closer Peter and Ivor grabbed a large banner and put it up in a gesture of defiance. On it the slogan 'No War' had been painted in giant letters. As if pre-arranged, protesters deployed themselves both alongside and behind it, facing down two lines of riot cops as they continued to move in. Things were getting tense, the atmosphere was charged. Mirko began leading a chant using a megaphone and as one we stood our ground.

The cops got to around twenty feet from us and stopped. Their commander stepped forward and asked to speak to the main organizer. Peter quickly assumed the role. Handing over his side of the banner to someone else, he stepped forward to listen to what the officer had to say. He returned to our ranks about ten minutes later, took the megaphone from Mirko and addressed the crowd.

'Brothers and sisters,' he announced, 'the police have just informed me that unless we disperse they will begin breaking up this protest using force. Now I don't about you, but based on this development I think we need to consider our position. One protest alone will not stop this criminal war. We need to be out in the streets again and again for our voices to be heard. With this in mind, I suggest that we end this demonstration, resolved to continue the struggle until the war ends and the troops are brought home!'

People in the crowd exchanged confused looks and snippets of conversation in response. This initial period of confusion lasted around five or ten seconds, before the first dissenting voice rang out.

'Bullshit!'

It was immediately followed by others, until within just a few seconds a chorus of derision and dissent filled the air in the form of the chant - 'Bullshit! Bullshit!'

There can be no worse feeling than being rejected by your peer group, and for a political activist of over thirty years it could only have been tantamount to a personal catastrophe. Peter was a man in his sixties, while those chanting bullshit at him were young and untouched as yet by the experience of defeat and disappointment, filled instead not just with the determination and desire to change the world, but also with the expectation that it could and would be changed. By relaying the orders of the cops to the crowd, in their eyes Peter had unwittingly changed from the leader of a demonstration against the war into an agent of the authority they despised. I felt sorry for him. He'd suddenly been plunged into a difficult situation and had taken the action he had with good intentions.

The demo ended, though in some disarray. It was right that it did because the cops would certainly have waded in and people would have been hurt. But with these things it's important that it ends in the right mood. Unfortunately in this case, for the reasons described, it did not.

As people dispersed I helped to pack everything away. By the time I got back to the car and began the drive home along Wilshire to Santa Monica, passing through Beverly Hills on my way back to Hollywood, I was exhausted, mentally and emotionally drained. In just this twenty-minute drive the deep and repugnant contradiction that lay at the heart of this society was laid bare. Extreme wealth and luxury sat side by side with extreme poverty and misery. On one side of Santa Monica Boulevard huge mansions and citadels of ostentation were protected by the cops and private security companies. On the other side you had an army of homeless people, poor immigrants mostly from South and Central America, and a legion of others struggling on the margins. It was a strange time. As the largest air attack since the Vietnam War was being unleashed on towns and cities in Iraq, using missiles and bombs with names such as the MOAB (Mother Of All Bombs) and Daisy Cutters, ordnance of unparalleled magnitude, people were going about their business as if nothing out of the ordinary was taking place. Hollywood parties, awards shows and movie premieres continued to take place every other night, events at which celebrities conspicuously wore Stars and Stripes pin badges on their lapels and went out of their way to praise the military, the young men and women from predominately poor backgrounds who none of them in truth cared the slightest fuck about.

Journalism in America was officially extinct as a profession. The people reporting from Iraq, the news readers in the studios, the pundits and commentators, all were unworthy of the title journalist or news correspondent. Instead they were propaganda mouthpieces for the Bush administration, cheerleaders for war and militarism. The patriotism and nationalism that had the nation in its grip was nauseating. I would soon find it near impossible to talk to anyone without getting embroiled in a debate or argument over the war. In fact, describing it as a war was a gross misrepresentation. It was slaughter, an attack by the world's superpower on a beleaguered and defenceless people.

But ultimately it does you no good to walk around in a constant state of turmoil. In the words of Joe Hill, the great American labor organizer, just before he was executed for standing up for the rights of working men and women to be treated like human beings and not animals at the turn of the last century: 'Don't mourn, organize.'

And with those words and this sentiment in mind I literally threw myself into antiwar work. Every morning, rising early, I would head straight over to the office. I was usually first to arrive. The place was always a tip from the previous day and I would spend the first twenty minutes or so cleaning up. Frank usually arrived around ten, always with a cup of coffee in his hand, and Peter would turn up around the same time having quit his job as a nurse so he could give the movement his full focus. We would sit and plan the day ahead, working out what needed to be done, etc., then set about doing it. Various other volunteers would pop in and out throughout the day, and invariably there would be new people coming in to inquire about getting involved. Ivor and Mandy were there most evenings after working a full day as lawyers at their respective offices in downtown LA. Hank was also constantly around, as were Mirko and Alan, with Millie and Joe Park never far away either. In other words, the place was buzzing.

It is only with the benefit of hindsight that you realize just how special and unique a certain period in your life was. This is certainly the case when I think back to those days in 2003 just after the war began. The sense of purpose and importance behind what we were doing was like nothing I've ever experienced, producing an energy that lifted me beyond anywhere I'd ever been before in terms of personal fulfilment and satisfaction. Of course, it was a contradictory feeling given the tragedy unfolding in Iraq, but everyone involved as volunteers in the LA branch of the ANSWER Coalition believed that every hour spent organizing against the war made a difference.

Every night there was a meeting, film or a class to attend. When I wasn't at the office or out manning stalls, handing out leaflets, flyposting, etc., you would invariably find me at a coffee shop in and around Hollywood reading and studying the works of Marx, Lenin, Trotsky, Che, poring over books by Eduardo Galeano, Noam Chomsky, and other radical thinkers. I read about the giants of American radicalism, the likes of the Chicago Martyrs, the Wobblies, Eugene Debs, Emma Goldman, John Reed, and so on. I studied the writings and speeches of Malcolm X, the Panthers, George Jackson, and other black radicals and revolutionaries. There I'd be, seated in a coffee shop on Sunset Boulevard, surrounded by a phalanx of wannabe screenwriters, actors, and filmmakers, engrossed in the aforementioned radical works, the diametric opposite of everything Hollywood stood for and the values it espoused.

I recall on one occasion, seated in the corner of a place I went to regularly, reading my way through a history of the Paris Commune when Nicole Kidman walked in with a a couple of others and sat down two or three tables away. It was surreal.

As far as my own ambitions regarding a career in Hollywood were concerned, by now I couldn't be less interested. Whenever Central Casting contacted me about a booking my reaction was always the same – dread. I'd come to loathe being on a set or a soundstage. Whereas at one time just walking onto Warner Bros, Paramount, Sony, or any of the other studio lots seemed the most exciting thing in the world, it now left me cold.

The first official mass demonstration after the war on Iraq began came in the middle of April. US troops had just taken Baghdad and within the group there was much trepidation over the impact it would have on numbers when it came to the demo. It was impossible to gauge in advance and nobody knew what to expect. The Bush administration, through its lackeys in the mainstream media, was diligently spreading the message that everyone should support the troops; that regardless of your views on the war it was time to lay those views aside and get behind 'our boys' who were putting their lives on the line for freedom and democracy. Of course it was complete nonsense, but nonetheless effective nonsense that many bought into. More disappointing was the fact that many on the left bought into it as well. Turning up on the corner of Hollywood and Vine, the assembly point for the demonstration, it was immediately obvious that a monumental degeneration had taken place. On February 15 some 70,000 had turned up to march along the same route. Today, just under two months later, the turnout was a tiny fraction of that.

We marched regardless, banners flying high, along Hollywood Boulevard. The crowds of pedestrians, unlike previous marches, were noticeably withdrawn. There was no waving or shouts of encouragement; instead the odd insult was directed our way. I noticed an abundance of stars n' stripes flags along the route. They were hung outside souvenir stores and hanging from windows all the way along. A pro-war counter demonstration had gathered at one of the intersections on the route and was making a lot of noise. As we passed them some of them had to be held back by the cops.

Strangely enough, rather than demoralized by this hostile reception, it made us even more determined. Instead of the broad heterogeneous movement of before now we were cohesive, coherent and focused. Those who remained in the movement from those heady days before the war began were the most advanced in terms of consciousness, understand that with the start of the war our work had only just begun.

Yet again the speeches went on way too long. Worse was the fact that many of them were woeful. At the very next organizing meeting I brought it up, citing the fact that the movement had shrunk significantly and urging that a more stringent criteria be put in place when it came to the speakers in order to maximize our effectiveness. It's fair to say that my argument went down like the proverbial lead balloon. Peter and Frank in particular were adamant that the current arrangement should remain in place regarding the speakers, as we were a broad movement and the first priority was to keep each of various organizations involved happy. They also rejected my assertion that the movement had shrunk. The problem lay with me and my own lack of analysis. Ivor was sat beside Peter nodding his head, just as he always did whenever he spoke. The only one who supported my view was Mirko. The others remained silent. I didn't know it then, but the seeds of the future split were being planted as the leadership turned inward.

18

But regardless of whether we acknowledged it or not, the fact the movement had taken a massive hit in terms of its size was inarguable. Completely unprepared for such an eventuality, initially we stumbled along like a blind man groping, repeating the same actions and activities that had served the movement so well before the bombs started dropping. This consisted of organizing demo after demo in the hope that people would return in their tens of thousands and all would be as before.

It soon became a demoralizing experience, attending meetings of only 15-20 people when just a few weeks before there would have been sixty and more, so many they could hardly all fit into the office; or in mass demos with only a few thousand, then hundreds, where before there'd been tens of thousands. In retrospect the leadership should have sat down to come up with a new way forward, one encompassing new ideas to take us forward. I felt it was time to change tack and start connecting the war in Iraq to the economic war being waged by the Bush administration against workers and the poor at home – the millions living in poverty, the millions more without healthcare, those who lived month to month, a paycheque away from the street in a society with no protection or safety net for those who fall through the cracks. Until this was done, this marrying of the war in Iraq with the war against the poor at home, it was clear to me that the movement would only consist of those who were involved as a result of moral choice and not material necessity.

Meanwhile, in Iraq US and British military forces seemed to be achieving their objectives with relative ease. As already mentioned, US forces had taken Baghdad, while the British had taken Basra with relative ease - at least judging by the reports being fed back to us. Like most information that comes via the corporate media, however, it was far from a complete picture of what was taking place. The Iraqi army and fedayeen volunteers, though poorly armed and equipped, had met the invasion of their country with desperate resistance. With no airforce, no navy, no communications systems to speak of, they had literally hurled themselves at the most lethal and powerful military ever seen, in places even managing to halt its advance. US military planners had decided on a strategy of speed and surprise, racing to take Baghdad while avoiding any direct engagement with opposition forces on the way to that objective if at all possible; the intent being to take care of any pockets of resistance after they'd first taken control of the capital.

Saddam and his sons, along with leading members of his regime, had gone underground with a price on their heads. The news pictures from Baghdad revealed a city and a country that had literally collapsed. Looting and lawlessness were now the order of the day, all committed out in the open as US troops stood by and watched. Government buildings and institutions, Saddam's palaces, the residencies of high-ranking members of the regime, museums containing priceless treasures and artefacts, they were all cleaned out in a wave of destruction not seen since the Mongol invasion of Baghdad in the 13th century. US Secretary of Defense, Donald Rumsfeld, when asked at a press conference about the wholesale looting of Baghdad, smiled and said: 'Stuff happens.'

The only facilities to do with the old regime that were protected by the invasion forces were those of the Oil Ministry and the Ministry of the Interior - evidence, if any were still needed, of the true motives behind the war.

Bush and his cohorts had been led to believe - by their own hubris and the word of various Iraqi exiles - that the invasion would be viewed by the vast majority of the Iraqi people as liberation from the tyranny of Saddam. In this they were soon to be proved mistaken. For hardly had Saddam's statue been unceremoniously pulled down (in a stunt later revealed to have been carried out by the US military and a small group of anti-Saddam former exiles) than a determined and effective resistance movement began hitting back at US military personnel, installations, and those Iraqis deemed collaborators with the occupation. The interim government was officially titled the Coalition Provisional Authority (CPA). It was headed up by US proconsul Paul Bremer, who was described as an expert on global terrorism. Bremer immediately set to work passing decrees and laws like a Roman governor from the days of another global empire. In short order he disbanded the Iraqi Army, made up of some 400,000 men, and then sent about dismantling the country's state-run economy and replacing it with a free-market alternative. The immediate beneficiaries of this were the multitude of Western corporations which like vultures around a dying carcass were lined up in anticipation of getting their hands on the contracts that were now up for grabs, especially in the fields of oil, security and reconstruction. Nothing, absolutely nothing, was done with the welfare of the Iraqi people in mind.

Two conferences were being organized by the movement. One was taking place in LA, the other in New York. The aim was to gather together activists from all over the country for a series of plenary sessions and workshops on the war, imperialism, capitalism and the various struggles against the same throughout history, hoping to extrapolate lessons and inspiration that we could use to take us forward. There were to be classes on Africa, Cuba and Latin America, Korea, and of course the Middle East. Major speakers from both within and without the organization were booked to attend for a series of morale-boosting speeches in an attempt to give the movement a much-needed shot in the arm.

I thought it was an excellent idea, as did most everyone else in the branch. Even Mirko and Alan were supportive and uncritical for once. As the West Coast conference was being held in LA the onus fell on us to organize and make it a success. Consequently, along with the other members of the group, I threw myself into the task of building what we hoped would be a fantastic weekend of political analysis, education and speeches. It turned out turned out to be everything we'd hoped and more. The conference was packed for the opening and closing plenary speeches, and the classes and various workshops enjoyed high turnouts. The most heartening aspect was the amount of young people in attendance, who'd been radicalized by the war. Now they were being educated, as well as educating themselves, on a whole range of topics connected to war and the economic system responsible for it. It was a beautiful thing to see them huddled together in groups throughout the venue and outside debating and discussing politics and ideas.

After the closing plenary, at which some of the speeches met with standing ovations, we all returned to Peter's house for a party. It was the perfect end to an almost-perfect day with everybody in high spirits. We were a strange combination - hardcore Marxists, committed liberals, disaffected Democrats, and faith-driven idealists of every age, demographic and ethnic group. And yet despite these differences in outlook and doctrine we remained a harmonious bunch, united by our desire to stop the war.

Of course, it couldn't last, and it didn't, but all the same I'll never forget the atmosphere of that night; the extent of the solidarity connecting us all in what was at bottom a microcosm of the society aspired to, even if in our own particular way.

During this period I was managing to make ends meet, though only just, by working as an extra a couple of days here and there in addition to the odd event working security. I mostly worked on two shows now, *Alias* and *Crossing Jordan*. *Alias* was marginally better to work on out of the two: it was shot at Disney while *Crossing Jordan* was shot at Universal. The facilities at Disney were better; it was a smaller studio lot and the food in the commissary was first class. Not so at Universal, a massive sprawling place where extras-holding was anywhere outside the soundstage and where the days were excruciatingly long.

Alias starred Jennifer Garner. In a departure from the norm she was courteous to everyone, including the extras, and radiated charm. I began on the show as an SE6 agent. These were the bad guys, part of a rogue intelligence agency whose objective was world domination. In this role, along with thirty or so others, I spent eight to ten hours a day walking back and forth behind and in-between the cast as they acted out their scenes - carrying files, pretending I was talking to other agents, or on the phone. In the second series of *Alias* I was cast as a CIA agent, one of the good guys, in a role that consisted of walking back and forth in behind and in-between the cast as they acted out their scenes – carrying files, pretending I was talking to other agents, or on the phone.

In other words, I was nothing more than a moving prop, utilized to make the background appear authentic. Occasionally, I was booked to work in a few of the show's external scenes, which was a pain in the arse as the location was usually miles away somewhere out in the Valley.

Alias was a show that liked to use various celebrities for guest starring roles. In my time there they had the likes of Faye Dunaway, Roger Moore, and Quentin Tarantino on the show. Faye Dunaway was legendary in the business for being difficult, and by the way she had her personal assistant scurrying around the place trying her best to cater to her every whim, I could see why. In contrast Roger Moore was the epitome of class, every bit the smooth and urbane character he is onscreen. It was a surreal moment when I was leaving the soundstage on my way to the toilet between set-ups one day and pushed open the door to find him standing on the other side on his way in. It struck as we passed one another that it's not often you come face to face with Roger Moore when you're on your way for a piss.

Tarantino is a great movie director but whoever told him he can act should be flung in jail. It was painful watching him try. He was playing a bad guy, a terrorist mastermind no less, but with that high pitched nasal voice of his, along with features that leave no doubt he's got the perfect face for radio, he'd be well advised to remain behind the camera.

One amusing experience on *Alias* came when Ricky Gervais guest-starred as a retired terrorist selling his services to the bad guys. Talk about miscasting. I was chosen to play one of the CIA guards who escort a handcuffed and hooded Gervais into the headquarters to be interrogated by Jennifer Garner et al. Throughout his time on the show, he kept laughing during his scenes and take after take had to be abandoned as a result. Things reached the point where the director and crew were tearing their hair out.

As far as screenwriting went, I'd more or less given up on the project I had in development with Tom and Jack at Pilot Films. Jack would call every so often to keep me abreast of things, informing me that so-and-so had turned it down, that he was sending it to such-and-such a producer or production company. The high point came when he managed to get the script to Sean Connery (there was a character in the story suitable for him) and I was called in to meet the producer who'd made it happen. She was an executive at the Jim Henson Company, the outfit behind the hugely successful *Muppets* television show and movies, and a personal friend it turned out of Scotland's most famous son. Her office was on the Henson studio lot on La Brea, not far from my apartment. She'd requested a meeting to discuss the script and so on yet another baking-hot day I made my way there, revelling in the privilege of being accorded a drive-on pass, which meant I was allowed to drive on and park in the studio lot next to the top of the range Bentleys and BMWs rather than out on the street with the rest of the hoi polloi. Who cared that I was doing so in an old Chevy Caprice that was belching smoke? Not I.

Sat in reception, it came as a surprise when I recognized the girl sent to escort me to the producer's office. Her name was

Judy. She had been the assistant bar manager at Las Palmas when I'd briefly worked security there. I remember I had a crush on her. Now here she was escorting me to her boss's office and offering me coffee. It was a moment to savour, if only for its karmic aspect, and it was hard not to smile in triumph.

Off she trotted to fetch my coffee, while I sat down on the comfy sofa in the office.

The producer's name was Julia, I'd say she was in her mid- to late-fifties, and as soon as we met she launched into a monologue praising the script, telling me she'd 'spoken to Sean' and he'd enjoyed it too. I sat there basking in her compliments as they fell from her lips one after the other like silver raindrops. She asked about my background and was most impressed when I informed her that it was very similar to Sean's - Scottish working class. I laid it on thick, even adjusting my accent to suit. She must have bought it, because suddenly she announced that she was going to 'call Sean at home in the Bahamas to see if he might be available to meet with me in person when he's in town in a couple of weeks for the Oscars.'

He was presenting one of the awards that year.

She had Judy get him on the line and went to speakerphone, I could tell, so that I could hear him say 'hello' in that distinctive voice of his before she took it off speakerphone and began firing questions at him about the script.

I walked out of her office twenty minutes later convinced I'd made it. Sean Connery would star in my movie, it would be lauded by the critics, and the doors to the kingdom of Hollywood would be thrown open for me to walk through. He hadn't given a definite no or yes when Julia had asked him about meeting with me when he was in town for that year's Oscars ceremony. Instead he said he would check his schedule and get back to her. No matter, as I walked across the Jim Henson studio lot towards my car it was all I could do to stop myself skipping across the tarmac.

But by the time I started the engine any sense of euphoria had been replaced by guilt. The carnage taking place in the Middle East was of far greater importance than my own narrow conceits and ambitions. Was it possible to combine both? Wasn't there the risk that I would abandon politics if and when that elusive door to success in Hollywood opened up?

I drove to a coffee shop, ordered a latte, and settled down at a corner table with a book. My phone went. It was Peter. He wanted to know if I was coming to New York for the East Coast antiwar conference in two weeks' time. If I was he would book my place now. Without any hesitation, I told him yes. The conference was being held the same weekend as the Oscars. By flying to New York I was ending any possibility of meeting Sean Connery. My dilemma was over. Political activism was the most important thing to me now. Fuck Hollywood.

19

Activists within the movement based in New York were putting people up who were arriving from out of town for the conference, but thinking about it Hank and I decided it would be preferable to pay for accommodation close to the venue in Manhattan rather than sleep on somebody's couch way out in Queens or Brooklyn. While searching online, I came across self-catering apartments located in Midtown Manhattan which slept two and worked out at just forty bucks a night each. I called and booked one for two nights.

The group were travelling to New York on separate flights at different times. Hank and I took the Friday night red-eye flight from LAX to JFK. On the way we discussed everything from the state of the world, the antiwar movement, various individuals in the group, and our respective backgrounds. Hank, a full-blooded Texan and proud, was very much a liberal, a man whom I've already mentioned believed wholeheartedly in the Constitution and America's role as leader of the free world. Bush and the neocons had subverted the Constitution and if only they could be removed from office and replaced by a good guy then everything in the garden would be rosy again.

It struck me listening to him that Hank had not been radicalized one bit as a result of his participation in the antiwar movement. Most of the other activists had become radicalized to varying degrees but not him. Surprising me even more was the vehemence with which he criticized the leadership. He literally tore into them, accusing them of incompetence and a lack of effectiveness, slating their radical views and calling them out for attacking the troops when we should in his opinion be getting behind 'our boys' while they were putting their lives on the line in Iraq.

I disagreed with him, I have to say, especially as the attacks on the troops he'd just cited had not taken place. On the contrary, when it came to the troops the approach from the beginning had been to support them by demanding they be brought home safe to their families, where they belonged.

Sitting listening to him, I was intrigued as to what Hank's reasons were for going to the conference at all. His reply was something about wanting to see if the movement had a plan for moving forward, and that if not, or if it wasn't to his liking, he would leave.

The reason I go into this incident in such detail is that it describes the confusion which many were experiencing at this juncture. The days of the mass demos were long gone, and the movement had failed to adapt to that reality. People like Hank, who'd remained but who weren't sold on the analysis that the problem lay in the system and not abuse of the system, literally did not know which way to turn. The next presidential election was due to take the following year, so it wasn't as if they could look to that for any kind of comfort or hope in the short term. This left them with an antiwar movement they were clearly dissatisfied with, which in the case of Hank had become a source of inner turmoil.

Moreover, as he'd alluded to in his comments to me over his reasons for being less than happy with the way things were headed, a major factor in this inner turmoil was the gnawing feeling that in supporting a movement that was trying to end a war involving the US and US troops, we were anti-American.

But how could anyone be anti-American when we're talking about the country that produced John Brown and the abolitionist movement against slavery, the country that gave the world the Wobblies, Eugene Debs, John Reed, the Abraham Lincoln Brigade that fought fascism in Spain, the men and women who'd stood firm in the face of McCarthyism, the Civil Rights Movement, Malcolm X, and so on? To be anti-American was to be ignorant of the history of those great progressive movements and champions of social justice which America had spawned.

On a certain level I couldn't help feeling that Hank's problem was that he lacked an understanding of this strand of American history. It wasn't readily available, and certainly not something you'd find in the mainstream historical narratives that were regurgitated endlessly. But it was there all the same if you looked for it.

We landed at JFK on a cool overcast morning, jumped in a cab, and sat back to enjoy the ride into Manhattan. The number of US flags flying from vehicles, windows and buildings was impressive. New York is where the tragic events of 9/11 had become immortalized and travelling the city from the airport it was apparent how significant the impact had been even two years later.

The apartment we'd booked was clean and spacious. The entire building was owned by three Irish guys who rented its apartments for short stays and weekend breaks. As soon we got settled in Hank and I had a quick bite to eat and some much needed coffee before leaving to make our way downtown for the opening of the conference. New York as a city is the diametric opposite of LA. With crowded sidewalks, valleys of skyscrapers, and so much frenetic activity, it possesses a vibrancy that's absent in LA. It's plain to see why New Yorkers hold both themselves and their city in such high regard. LA may have year-round sunshine, but apart from that it's hard to see what distinguishes it compared to its East Coast counterpart.

Just making our way on the subway downtown, soaking up the sights and sounds of the Big Apple, was an experience in itself. I almost forgot about the conference as I soaked up the mayhem and activity unfolding around me. I recalled the great anarchist Emma Godman's autobiography *Living My Life* with its evocative description of life in New York's slums in the late nineteenth and early twentieth century. I thought about the books I'd read by Henry Miller, another great writer from New York who'd left the city for Paris in the late twenties. In *Tropic of Cancer* Miller writes: *'New York is cold, glittering, malign. The buildings dominate. There is a sort of atomic frenzy to the activity going on; the more furious the pace, the more diminished the spirit. A constant ferment, but it might just as well be going on in a test tube. Nobody knows what it's all about. Nobody directs the energy. Stupendous. Bizarre. Baffling. A tremendous reactive urge, but absolutely uncoordinated.'*

Absorbing its atmosphere and madness it was no wonder that New York had produced such great writers and literature. Studying my fellow passengers riding the subway downtown, I noticed the weary countenances and forlorn facial expressions of people struggling to get by. It then hit me that the excitement and dynamism which New York City was associated with the world over was just as much a myth as it was when applied to LA and Hollywood. The reality for the majority in both cities was a perennial struggle to survive.

In the end the conference proved a disappointment. I had fully expected it to be much better attended and more inspiring than it turned out. Parts of the country were suffering severe snow blizzards, and as a result many of the delegates had been forced to cancel. That's what the organizers were saying anyway. I wasn't entirely convinced though. To me it was merely further proof that things had contracted to the point where we could no longer be seriously or accurately described as a mass movement.

Still, we had a blast anyway. The high point came on the second night, when a group of us hit a few bars close to the venue. There's an Irish pub in downtown Manhattan that will never forget the night a large group of peace activists took it over. We repeatedly burst into song, mostly drunken and loud renditions of *The Internationale*. Somebody said the four or five big guys at the bar who kept shooting dirty looks in our direction were off-duty cops. As soon as we heard this we turned the volume up a notch to piss them off even more.

20

Gabriel called out of the blue one day to see if I was looking for work. He'd been hired to organize security for movie premieres and one off events at the El Capitan movie theater on Hollywood Boulevard. His call could not have come at a more propitious time. Financially things were tight (they were always tight), and despite my earlier pledge to never work security again, I immediately took him up on the offer.

The El Capitan was owned by the Disney Corporation, a disgusting company to work for in that they treated their employees no better than cannon fodder, paying poverty wages while demanding robotic standards of performance and commitment. As for things like health insurance, pension or labor rights, you must be having a laugh. When it came to Disney the aforementioned only existed in the pages of science fiction novels.

Working as a freelance security contractor for Disney was nowhere near as bad as being one of their employees though. The pay was significantly better for one thing, and the various managers and supervisors treated you with more respect than they did their regular staff. Regardless, it was still a shitty gig which involved standing around in a stiff suit looking on as a procession of celebrities and movie stars paraded in front of the public and assembled press like latter-day divinities. Typically we would begin in the afternoon as the final touches to the set were being added and the red carpet rolled out. Every movie had a theme that was reflected in the set erected for its premiere, and no expense was spared when it came to making sure it looked impressive. At the back of the theater a giant marquee was also set up to host the after-party, housing the kind of catering operation you would expect to find at a luxury hotel.

Around a dozen of us freelancers, hired by Gabriel, were

deployed at strategic points around the event. We'd been selected as a result of our physical presence (we were all over 6ft in height) and placed in the front line. My normal position at these events was at the end of the red carpet where the limos disgorged their cargo of celebrities to begin the customary walk along the line of the assembled international press and paparazzi. We were organized and expected to be imbued with the purpose of a military operation, primed to carry out our duty of making sure the invited guests and celebrities were cocooned and pandered to, protected from the spectators and fans that were always guaranteed to be gathered on both sides of the street in considerable number. The entire process of greeting the invited VIPs as they arrived and escorting them along the red carpet and on into the theater took a couple of hours. After this part was over a crew of construction workers would immediately begin dismantling the set and rolling up the red carpet, placing it in storage until the next premiere came round. At this point we abandoned the front of the theater for the back, ready to escort the guests to the marquee for the after-party as soon as the movie ended.

Once all the guests had been successfully escorted to the party, it was time for us to let our hair down, even though we weren't supposed to. One of the things I liked about Gabriel was the fact he didn't take himself or security work seriously. With his size and presence he could have been assured of a lucrative career as a bodyguard or head of security at any nightclub in Hollywood of his choosing. Instead, he scorned the very idea. As he saw it we were no better than lackeys for the rich and famous, and with the pride of a professional fighter running through his veins he never forgot it. His lack of respect for the job was demonstrated in the way he wandered around sneaking drinks and laughing and joking with the guys. Because of his size, he was accorded the most important task of walking the red carpet with the guests, keeping a watchful eye in the background as they gave short interviews to the world's press and posed for pictures. But instead of adopting the poise and body language of a member of the special forces, as he was expected to, Gabriel thought nothing of standing there on his phone talking to girlfriends and friends, his free hand in his pocket, as if he was taking a stroll in the park.

It was the same when he worked as a limo driver for a spell, charged with transporting high-end clients around town. On one assignment he was sent out to the airport to pick up a world-famous rap artist and drive him to the Beverly Hills Hotel.

One of the gigs we worked for Disney involved providing personal security for various executives and assorted dignitaries during a party held to celebrate that season's list of TV shows the company was producing. Gabriel and I had to stand around watching the bastards gorge themselves on the best of food and expensive champagne in Wolfgang Puck's restaurant next to the Kodak Theater on Hollywood Boulevard, where they hold the Oscars every year.

After a while we said fuck it and started getting wired into the free food and champagne ourselves. In no time the two of us were drunk. I recall trying to stuff a slice of chocolate fudge cake into my mouth and getting it all over my white shirt. As I was trying to clean it off the live entertainment began. It was Tom Jones. As soon as he started singing *Delilah* I did the only thing I could under the circumstances – I called home to tell my mum.

Gabriel parked at the wrong terminal with the result that said rap artist was left wondering what the fuck had happened to his limo. When he received an irate call from the office inquiring as to his whereabouts, instead of apologizing and rushing to pick up the client at the correct place, he asked the office to pass the details *his* location to the client and get him to make his way to him. Then, later, driving his client around town, he failed to notice that he was low on gas and ended up running out, with the limo coming to a stop in the middle of the Hollywood Hills and his passenger pissed off in the back.

Another event we worked which illustrated his less than stellar attitude to a career in security was the annual Teamsters Convention, being held that year in Las Vegas. A small group of us were hired to spend the week making sure that the union's then leader, James Hoffa Jnr, was provided with round-the-clock protection. There'd been threats of violence as a result of an acrimonious split in the Teamsters over an upcoming leadership election, in which allegations of fraud and intimidation were being thrown back and forth between the rival candidates and their respective camps.

The convention was being held in the main ballroom of the Paris Hotel. This was a vast, grandiose place which boasted an exact recreation of the Hall of Mirrors at the Palace of Versailles, made famous during the reign of Louis XIV. The word vulgarity was invented for this establishment, not to mention Vegas as a whole. Regardless, most of the guys were looking forward to sampling the famous Las Vegas nightlife over the course of the week we were scheduled to be there. What none of us realized until arriving was that we'd be required to work 14-hour shifts. This meant that by the end of each shift we were too exhausted to do much more than grab a bite to eat and a couple of beers back at our decidedly downmarket hotel on the edge of town before falling into bed.

The long hours didn't stop Gabriel however.

Each night after the shift was over he arrived back at the hotel, showered, changed, and immediately ventured out again, returning drunk well after midnight to snatch a few hours sleep before having to get up for work again. I accompanied him one night and suffered for it the whole of the next day.

What made this job especially tiring was the fact that long bouts of boredom were interspersed with flashpoints of confrontation as rival factions of Teamsters (and they were big guys, believe me) squared off in the hotel and we had to get in between them before a mass brawl ensued. The big day came towards the end of the week when James Hoffa Jnr arrived to give the keynote speech. We were briefed to be on our toes. Hoffa had his own bodyguards, two of them, and our role would be to act as an extra security cordon backing them up. Both former cops, they arrived armed and pumped up ready for action. Gabriel was selected to be Hoffa's personal escort during his appearance at the convention in the expectation that his presence would deter any potential adversaries. Hoffa's own security meanwhile would remain in the background, mingling with the crowd in order to identify problems before they got a chance to manifest.

You might think that being selected for such an important role would have instilled a sense of diligence and professionalism in Gabriel. You'd be wrong. Instead, he kept wandering off to play the slot machines or to sneak a cocktail at the bar when he was supposed to be shadowing the leader of the biggest and most powerful labor union in America, one made famous by the original Jimmy Hoffa in the union's heyday as a result of his dealings with the mob and subsequent disappearance. But Gabriel couldn't give a monkey's about any of that, and when he was hauled up by Hoffa's personal security guys for his shitty attitude his response was to snort his disdain and play them with a perfunctory nod and a disparaging, 'Yeah, okay. I got it.'

The icing on the cake occurred during Hoffa's speech. Gabriel was posted backstage to make sure nobody tried to get back there who didn't belong. When he failed to respond to repeated radio checks we rushed to the backstage area to make sure he was all right. We arrived to find him sitting on a plastic chair, arms folded and chin on chest, snoring his head off.

The occupation of Iraq was now a fact of life. An antiwar movement that before the US invaded was large and buoyant was now dead on its feet, despite a valiant effort on the part of those still involved. To all intents and purposes the Iraqi people were on their own. The carnage being wrought in the developing world at the hands of the developed world, which began with Christopher Columbus' first expedition to the Americas back in the fifteenth century, was continuing unabated at the start of the 21st. The vast majority of people living in the West, whose governments were responsible for continuing this ignoble legacy, trustees of an economic system dripping in blood from head to foot, were apathetic in the face of these crimes, though mostly through a lack of awareness as a result of a supine media. The primary role of those on the far left of the political spectrum was to work to impart the consciousness required for action, to instil the belief that the people could make a difference, just as history has proved more than once.

But for all that the far left had encountered way more defeats than victories in its history, and along the way had demonstrated a propensity to acrimonious splits and internal feuds in response to these defeats, rendering it weak and divided. It was a tradition that had taken root within the LA branch of the ANSWER Coalition by the middle of 2004.

Now weekly organizing meetings at the office, designed to plan the next week's activities and actions, were reduced to a forum whereby the activities and work already undertaken by one faction within the group was reported back to the rest as a fait accompli. Thus, typically, Peter would casually announce that Ivor was booked to do a radio interview, Mandy to speak at a union meeting, while he was scheduled to attend a Palestine solidarity event representing the organization.

No one seemed willing to question this development. When I attempted to at one meeting I was made to feel like a pariah, accused of being 'uncomradely'. From that moment my ostracization was assured. I remained a while longer, suffering through meetings that were now merely a prelude to the split that everybody knew was coming. Alan had already decided to walk away, while Mirko joined me in deciding to stay and try to ride it out. It couldn't last, however, and neither could we.

Just prior to the split, which involved one faction letting themselves into the office late one night and removing most of the files, computers and other equipment, Alan and I decided it was time to depart.

After just a few weeks I no longer missed being politically active. Instead it hit me that in the past few months I'd spent more time focused on internal office politics than trying to build a mass movement. The sense of liberation and lightness I now experienced more than compensated for any sense of sadness at leaving a cause I had been dedicated to over the past few years. No meaningful challenge was being mounted to the Bush administration at all by this point anyway, with the few thousand stalwarts who formed the backbone of the US antiwar movement and had stayed the course now reduced to doing nothing more than bearing witness.

In the immediate aftermath I returned to the cause of trying to re-establish my previous career as a Hollywood extra and stand-in, else be faced with the prospect of being unable to pay the rent and ending up homeless. This proved more difficult than I thought, as by this point I had myself a reputation as a trouble-maker. My file over at Central Casting contained a long list of complaints filed against me by the various productions I'd worked on. These infractions included walking off the set, refusing to comply with instructions, getting into arguments with crew members, and bad timekeeping. I could not disagree that my attitude to the industry and the job was not good. No matter how hard I tried I just couldn't accept a state of affairs whereby you were expected to allow yourself to be treated like a dog - shouted at, insulted, pushed around (metaphorically and, on occasion, physically), and denied the right to dignity. Of course, you had the option of falling back on the tired excuses employed by many to justify accepting this treatment - 'paying your dues' for example - but I had long since rejected that line of thinking.

As for Tom and Jack and the project I had in development with them, I took the decision not to renew our agreement at the end of the third year. It was clear by now that it wasn't going anywhere, and despite doing rewrite after rewrite I was yet to be paid a penny for my efforts. I broke the news to Jack via email, anxious to ensure there was no acrimony involved. I liked him regardless of the lack of results with the script, and over the past couple of years we'd become friends. We'd been out socializing a few times and I'd been round to his house more than once. Despite the fact we hailed from different sides of the tracks – he the product of an Oxbridge education and UCLA, me what you would call in Scotland a schemie and about as far from Oxbridge as it was possible to be – I found him to be a gentleman. Tom and I on the other hand clashed, and by the end the two of us were barely able to mask our mutual disdain. I admired and respected his work ethic and commitment, but that was all. It was as well we parted company and went our separate ways.

Anyway, Jack seemed to accept my decision not to renew our agreement with no hard feelings and the matter was settled.

Or at least that's what I thought.

While aimlessly browsing the web one afternoon a few months later, out of nothing more than benign curiosity to see what they were up to, I looked at their website. On it was listed their current development slate, comprising those projects they were in the process of developing. When I saw they had a project currently being developed in conjunction with Miramax that was very similar in terms of the story and characters to the one I'd had with them, I couldn't believe it. They'd stolen my idea.

Pissed off, I scanned the Yellow Pages and called up a few entertainment attorneys at random. After speaking to three or four, I happened upon one that after listening to the case expressed a willingness to represent me on a contingency basis - in other words, no win no fee. Their offices were located in downtown LA and I drove down to meet with them that Sunday afternoon. The firm was owned by two Egyptian brothers. They were young and having just started their own law firm, they were also hungry, hence the reason they were in the office on a Sunday. What attracted them to my case was the involvement of Miramax, owned by the ubiquitous and larger-than-life Weinstein brothers. Formidable characters, at the time they were feared within the industry, notorious for being ruthless in their dealings with everyone from the major studios to writers, actors and directors. They'd enjoyed enormous success with a variety of projects, many of them innovative, and they seemed bullet proof. As my Egyptian lawyers told me, with Miramax's involvement the stakes were raised considerably, offering the possibility of a big settlement if we managed to bring a successful lawsuit.

I left that initial meeting satisfied that justice was going to be served. A month or so later I called the office for an update to be informed that Amir, the younger of the two partners, and the one responsible for taking on my case, had collapsed and died of an aneurism. As a result his brother Muhammad had decided to close the firm.

Yet again fate had conspired against me.

Later I would come round to the conclusion that I had probably been mistaken in accusing Tom and Jack of ripping off my script. Within the movie business there are so many scripts flying around that inevitably many bear a similarity to others. In fact it is well nigh impossible to write a completely original story when you consider that every story written, even made, has already been told in one way or another. Jack I strongly believed then and still do now was not someone who would rip off another writer's work. But such was my mindset at the time, I really did believe I'd been wronged. Twas ever thus.

21

But things weren't all doom and gloom, for it was around this time that I met Laura.

The Cat & Fiddle was a British pub on Sunset Boulevard and something of a Hollywood institution. It was popular with various British actors and celebrities, who either lived in LA or were in town on business. Weekend nights were always packed with a combination of Brits and Americans who appreciated British music, beer, and culture. They also did a good lunch here, and on those rare occasions when I was flush I would come down and enjoy one in the patio while leisurely perusing one of the British newspapers that were always lying around. I recall being intrigued to learn that the building in which the pub was housed, a grand affair in a Spanish style, had once been the home of Hollywood legend Rudolph Valentino. Such trivia about the history of buildings and streets in Hollywood gave them their magic and every time I was in the Cat & Fiddle thereafter I thought about old Rudolph, a man with a reputation for shagging everything that moved, and what Hollywood must have been like during its golden age.

So on this particular night, a Thursday, Kenny and I ventured out for a few drinks. I first met Kenny when I briefly worked as a production assistant on the daytime TV show *Diagnosis Murder*, starring Dick Van Dyke. I was covering for the regular guy, Marcus, whom I'd met on the show when I worked a few days on it as an extra and we got talking. Though he worked as a PA, Marcus had acting ambitions and had won himself a small part in an independent film. The only problem was that the three days he was scheduled to work on the film clashed with his regular job on *Diagnosis Murder*. He was desperate to find someone to cover for him as a consequence, and when he told me I instantly saw an opportunity for a few days work at a higher rate of pay than that of an extra. So I told him I had experience of working as a PA and would be happy to help him out. I was lying of course. I had zero experience of working as a PA. But this was Hollywood, a town and an industry which invented the art of lying.

Anyway, the upshot was that Marcus recommended me to the Second AD, who was Kenny, and I got the job.

The experience taught me that working as a production assistant on a TV show or on a movie is even more monotonous and soul-destroying than working as an extra, involving as it does long interminable days on your feet at the beck and call of every other member of the crew.

Kenny had spent time studying in the UK on a scholarship and was something of an Anglophile. He'd moved to LA from Chicago with the ambition to direct and by the time we met had made an independent film that never managed to catch fire or open any doors. What it did do was leave him broke and in debt, and as a result he was forced to return to work as a Second AD, which he'd done for ten years by this point and hated with a passion. We kept in touch after my brief stint on the show and would meet up for coffee or a drink every so often, where invariably the topic of conversation would be movies and the industry in general.

Our previous night out had been memorable for all the wrong reasons. Kenny had just acquired a new car, was keen to take it out for a spin, and invited me to go with him. It was a Saturday night and we decided to head down the coast. We arrived at Redondo Beach to find it jam-packed. Outside every bar a long line of people stood waiting to get in. Purely by chance as we were heading out, having decided to abandon the idea and drive back to Hollywood, I saw a place that looked promising. It was a nightclub where you could see inside from the street as a result of the large glass windows that ran its entire length. Though the place looked busy there weren't that many waiting to get in.

Kenny parked the car in the lot just along the street and we took a wander down. Ten minutes later we were inside having our first drink. It was a strange crowd - all the girls seemed to be dressed in lingerie and the guys in tight-fitting vests and T-shirts, sporting physiques which suggested they ate steroids for breakfast, lunch and dinner. It turned out we'd stumbled on the launch party for some new men's magazine.

Kenny and I were clearly out of place. We were were half the size of the majority of the guys and dressed in normal clothes. We looked like a couple of nerds by comparison. Fuck it. As long as we could have a couple of drinks we were happy.

About half an hour into proceedings I was standing on one side of a table by the door which led out to the smoking patio. Kenny was sitting on the other side telling me about the girl he'd just been dancing with, when all of a sudden I lurched forward and almost fell over the table on top of him. One of the muscle guys had pushed me aside as he made his his way out to the smoking patio leading a girl by the hand. As he passed I quickly recovered, leaned over and gave him a small push in the back. He stopped, turned and came right up to my face.

'Hey, man, I was just tryin' to get by ya. Don't make a big thing outta of it, okay?'

He pushed me again, before turning and resuming his walk with the girl following behind. I leaned forward and gave him another poke in the back. He turned again, let go of the girl, and came forward - this time with bad intentions.

I was ready and caught with him with a right hand on the way in. He stumbled back, holding his nose, which was bleeding. I put the drink I was holding in my left hand down on the table and faced him. He was a big man, huge shoulders and arms, and looking at him my arse started flapping. I'm dead, I remember thinking. This bastard's going to kill me.

But instead of that he started shouting for security. It was time to leave. I quickly motioned to Kenny and we started heading for the door. We passed three of the bouncers on the way as they ran past us to the scene. We reached the door and had just made it outside past another three bouncers, when the message came through on their radios to stop us leaving, whereupon they immediately surrounded us. The big guy appeared, pointing at me and shouting the odds, demanding the bouncers detain me until the cops arrive as I'd just assaulted him. I told the bouncers that he was obviously mistaken. Someone had hit him but it wasn't me, I said. I pointed out the size of the guy compared to me and told them I was just a tourist and that I was scared and wanted to go home.

'All right,' the one in charge said. 'Go. Get the fuck outta here.'

As they ushered the big guy back into the club, still pointing at me and shouting, Kenny and I began walking double time in the direction of the car. Reaching the parking lot, and just when I was starting to think we were home free, I glanced back and saw the big guy running along the street in our direction. For some reason he'd taken his shoes and socks off and was in his bare feet.

'Motherfucker! You motherfucker! You're fuckin' with a Navy Seal, man! You're fuckin' with a Seal!'

He came at me swinging. I reached over his punches to grab him by the hair and get him down. In the process I caught a couple in the mouth. His hair was short but I hung on regardless. I could taste the blood in my mouth from the punches I'd taken and I could not afford to take any more. He kept struggling and shouting, 'Don't fuck with the Seals! You're fuckin' with a Seal!'

I didn't think he was a Navy Seal.

Three of the bouncers from the club arrived just as my arms were starting to ache from the strain of holding him down. I'd never been as glad to see anyone. They broke it up and told me and Kenny to scram as they kept the big guy back. We jumped in the car and took off. As we rolled out of the parking lot he was screaming and shouting that I was getting away. I waved. He didn't wave back.

But getting back to the Cat & Fiddle, Kenny and I were enjoying a few beers on this warm Thursday night. We decided to move from the bar out to the patio, which was busy by this point, and almost immediately I noticed a tall girl with red hair standing among a small group. I was sure I recognized her from somewhere. She was attractive and every time I glanced over she seemed to be smiling and laughing. Two beers later I moved in. The other two girls with her melted into the background as I asked her if we'd met somewhere before. She laughed while saying that for an opening line this was a crap. She was British and I liked her straight away. Kenny had began chatting to one of her friends and we spent the rest of the night in their company.

Laura, though originally from the UK, had been living in LA for ten years, where she worked as a journalist for newspaper back in the UK. She was refreshingly down to earth and lived in a small house in West Hollywood on a quiet street that was in stark contrast to Sycamore Avenue, where I lived. Here there were no homeless trudging up and down, no drug dealers or crack addicts, no police choppers circling overhead, and no chaotic traffic and crowds at the weekend. Here it was just peace, quiet, and tranquillity. Pretty soon I was spending every weekend there.

Part of Laura's job included going to movie screenings. I would often accompany her and afterwards we'd go to the Kings Road Café on Beverly Boulevard, where over coffee and a snack we would sit and dissect the movie we'd just seen. They were great times, easily the best I'd experienced since moving to LA four years previously.

It was also around this period that Arnold Schwarzenegger was elected Governor of California, after a recall initiative had succeeded in forcing an early election. The incumbent, Gray Davis, was a Democrat, while Arnold was an avowed Republican.

The fact that a movie star could be elected to such high office was indicative of the times and of the role and power of celebrity in the land of the free. Back when I'd been obsessed with lifting weights as a teenager, Arnold had been my idol. His rags to riches story had been an inspiration, as had his self-belief and determination to reach the very top.

Fifteen years later this was no longer the case. Now, far from being my idol, he represented everything I detested. This was confirmed when one of his first decisions as governor was to deny a petition for clemency by Kevin Cooper, a black death-row inmate at San Quentin penitentiary, whose case had been the catalyst for a campaign to save his life based on evidence suggesting that his conviction for murder eighteen years earlier may have been unsafe. Deciding that I couldn't stand by while a many who may well be innocent was murdered by the state, I began attending Save Kevin Cooper campaign meetings, which culminated in a protest outside Schwarzenegger's massive and opulent mansion compound at the bottom of Sunset, close to Malibu. For me it was a seminal moment, an exercise in expunging one of the false idols of my youth. It was made more so by the fact that among Schwarzenegger's security team keeping an eye on us was Brian, the guy who'd shown me the ropes at Sombrero's, the Mexican nightclub and restaurant on the Universal Citywalk where I'd briefly worked security a few years earlier.

Cooper's execution, scheduled to take place a week or so later, was postponed just a few hours before in order to allow for more DNA testing. As I write this he is still on death row fighting to establish his innocence and save his life.

Other aspects of my life had remained more or less the same. After El Capitan, Gabriel was made head of security at a new nightclub on Hollywood Boulevard called The Ivar. Owned by a consortium of South African businessmen the place was huge, consisting of two levels, four bars, two VIP lounges, and a massive dance floor. Gabriel offered me a job and with no other source of income I accepted. The place was so big it employed twenty guys to work the security every week night with an additional five on weekends.

I arrived for the initial security meeting just before the opening night, convened to allow everyone who'd been hired to meet the managers and each other. Here we go again, I thought. I'd been to more of these meetings in the past four years than I cared to recall. As with the others, I spent this one standing at the back doing my best to conceal my complete disinterest. The security operations manager was a guy who went by the name of Oscar. He was tiny; in fact he was so small he looked like he slept in an incubator. He was supposed to be a karate expert, and the rumour among the guys was that despite his diminutive stature he could break a man's arm with one handstrike. I recall him coming into the club drunk with a group of friends on his night off a couple of weeks down the line. He decided to show me some moves and had me put my arm out. He began chopping it with his hand to demonstrate his power. I've never been tickled so hard in all my life.

Anyway, at this initial security meeting, Gabriel stood alongside Oscar as he went over the usual list of security do's and don'ts, making him look silly by comparison.

My heart sank when the meeting ended and a large box of T-shirts was produced. These, we were informed, along with a pair of black trousers and black shoes, constituted our uniform. The T-shirts were plain black with the word SECURITY emblazoned across the front and back in big yellow letters. My immediate reaction was to balk at having to wear such undignified attire. What was wrong with the usual dark suit? At least dressed in a suit you could hold your head up and attain a semblance of respect from the customers. Dressed in a cheap, ill-fitting black T-shirt with the word SECURITY on it respect and dignity would instantly be rendered words from a foreign language.

As the rest of the guys stepped forward to grab one from the box, I stood off to the side, struggling mightily with an enormous sense of anger at the situation and the dilemma I was suddenly faced with. It's difficult to explain, the extent and intensity of the sensitivity I felt over what most would probably consider a problem of false pride. The T-shirt in itself wasn't so the issue, it was what it represented. Simply put, it was a manifestation of the fact that after four years of struggling and striving to get somewhere as a screenwriter in Hollywood, I'd failed.

Gabriel saw me standing apart from the group looking less than happy. He came over to see what the problem was. When I told him I felt uncomfortable about wearing the T-shirt the club was providing, he immediately launched into an angry tirade in criticism of my, as he described it, 'shitty attitude.' I should think myself fortunate I had this job at all, he said, especially with my track record. He told me he'd had to use his influence with the manager to get me this gig and I should be grateful. He wound up his diatribe with a warning not to give him a hard time. He was head of security and he wasn't going to allow me or anybody else fuck it up for him.

He didn't wait for a reply and marched off imperiously, leaving me to chew over the verbal drubbing I'd just received. I was neither upset or offended. On the contrary, how could I be given that everything he'd just said was right? My mistake was in thinking I could resume working in this business while being utterly disdainful of it, thinking I could conceal my true feelings and endure for the sake of a paycheck. I couldn't.

There was no need to hang around and I quietly removed myself from both the place and the security business for good. As for Gabriel, we lost touch after that. I heard through the grapevine a few months down the line that he got fired for drinking on the job. He started work at another club in Hollywood shortly thereafter. While there he met an ex-stripper and moved in with her. She introduced him to cocaine and their relationship quickly became abusive. One night, after a bad fight,

Gabriel stormed out of the house and took her car for a drive. His own car was in the garage being repaired.

He'd been drinking and snorting coke, so had she, and as soon as he left she picked up the phone and called the cops to report that her car had just been stolen by a man who was driving under the influence. When the cops pulled Gabriel over on the freeway they discovered that not only was he driving under the influence, he was also driving without insurance. In addition, there were more than a few unpaid traffic tickets against his name. He spent the next two weeks as a guest of LA County Jail. Upon his release, he returned to the house to discover that his ex had moved out and emptied the place, taking the furniture, his clothes, everything. She'd also emptied his bank account, leaving him with nothing except his car, which was lucky as he had nowhere else to sleep. Former friends and acquaintances from the bar and club scene melted away, either making excuses for why they couldn't let him sleep on their couch or else avoiding his calls altogether. Realizing he was in an impossible situation, Gabriel made an SOS call to his mother in Sweden, who wired him the price of an air ticket home. The last I heard he was back in Malmo working in a bakery.

22

The autumn of 2004 and the nation's attention was focused on the upcoming presidential election between George W. Bush and Democratic Party candidate John Kerry. Despite his obvious flaws and a charisma bypass, Kerry carried the hopes of half a nation with him. California had for years been a traditional bastion of support for the Democratic Party and Kerry bumper stickers and posters were everywhere. With the war going so badly in Iraq, the massive spike in the deficit after one term of a Republican administration, Bush and the neocons unleashing an attack on civil liberties, the poor and the working class, its controversial policy of 'might is right' in international affairs, the disrespect it had shown to international institutions such as the United Nations, the complete denial of global warming as a consequence of human activity - with all of the aforementioned the stakes in this election could not be higher.

That said, the truth is both candidates were white, middle-aged, Yale-educated millionaires. Not only that but both sought to outdo the other in presenting themselves as cheerleaders for the US military, equally intent on seeing the 'mission' in Iraq through. In fact, one of Kerry's key campaign pledges was to send more troops if elected in order to get the job done.

Despite my justified cynicism, I sat riveted to the election debates with Laura. Seeing US democracy in action is quite an experience. It's exactly as the great American novelist, essayist, and cultural commentator Gore Vidal said:

'In America, if you want a successful career in politics, there is one subject you must never mention, and that is politics. If you talk about standing tall, and it's morning in America, and you press the good-news buttons, you're fine. If you talk about budgets, tax reform, bigotry, and so on, you are in trouble.'

The 2004 election confirmed another Vidal aphorism – namely

that America is a one-party state with two right wings.

In the end Kerry lost and Bush second term was assured. Hope vanished like air out of a burst ballon. All seemed lost.

Meanwhile, Laura managed to get me hooked up with a job in a paparrazi news agency based in Santa Monica. Splash News had been set up by two British guys and had grown to become the biggest in the business. They had offices in London, LA, Sydney, and Toronto, earning a reputation for being aggressive in what was a supremely aggressive business when it came to snatching celebrity pictures which in many cases sold for hundreds of thousands of dollars.

Their Santa Monica office was on Abbot Kinney Boulevard, a trendy street of antique shops, boutiques, second-hand bookstores, cafes, wine bars, and apartments that cost an arm and a leg to rent. I arrived for work on my first day without a clue what to expect. The interior of the office was even more impressive than the exterior. It was on two levels, open plan, and the people working there were dressed in trendy clothes. It was more like an ad agency than the office of a company which made a fortune out of invading other people's privacy, catching them in compromising situations, and fucking up their lives. What struck me most was the near-feral attitude towards celebrities which reigned. In fact, it would be fair to say that the central ethos of the company was an underlying hatred of the people they hunted and photographed, regarding them as no better than prey, vermin even. Given the nature of the business, I suppose such a mindset was key, else you wouldn't be able to do it. But still.

My first job consisting of sifting through piles of old newspapers and putting them in chronological order. I was allocated a small desk on the second level and went straight to work. Across from me was sat a woman who spent the entire day barking down the phone in a German accent trying to sell pictures to celebrity news outlets, magazines, and TV networks all over the world. She was very loud and her face would turn red as she negotiated a fee for each picture with great passion. It was like listening so someone negotiating the sale of their soul.

After three days I never went back.

This meant that towards the end of 2004 I found myself in the invidious position of having no income at the same time as I was no longer able to legally work in the States due the expiration of my visa. Laura and I talked it over. She'd been in the States long enough and was ready to move back to the UK, she told me. Her company was based in London anyway, which meant it wouldn't be a problem for her to relocate. The prospect of living in London appealed to me as well. Every time I'd visited the place I'd come away wishing I could have stayed longer. And so it was settled. London it was.

The only problem was that before Laura could move she would have to wait until her office organized a replacement and she had shown whoever it was the ropes. This process would take four months to complete. We were now into November, which meant the earliest she could leave was the following March. If I left now we were looking at waiting four months before seeing one another again. It was a hard thing to contemplate, and with each week that passed the relationship came under more strain as a result. I'd already had to ask the manager of my apartment building for some leeway regarding the rent, but her forbearance would not last longer than a month or two at most. Eventually I was forced to ask Laura if I could move in with her on the basis it would only be for a couple of weeks until I could organize my flight home. There I'd wait for her to join me over the Christmas and New Year period and after that until she returned for good the following March, when we'd relocate to London and set up home together as planned.

Laura agreed, though I'm sure with reservations about what it portended in terms of the relationship and my increasing dependency on her. I had my own reservations, especially as it had been quite some time since I'd lived with anyone. A part of me was reluctant to lose the autonomy which comes with that. But of course I had no choice, and fully aware that without Laura I'd be out on my arse, I was more than grateful.

The two weeks we agreed I'd be staying prior to moving in stretched to six. Throughout I focused my efforts on making a last-gasp attempt to get something going with my writing. Laura seemed perfectly happy about my extended stay. In fact, in terms of the relationship, things had never been better. We'd spend lazy mornings in bed together, go for long walks through Runyon Canyon, and out for breakfast or lunch at the little café we both liked at the bottom of her street. I may not have been sure what the future held in terms of a career, but by this point I was certain that Laura would be in that future come what may.

As the day of my departure from LA neared, gnawing regrets at leaving started to appear. All I'd known for the past five years had been the rarefied environment of Hollywood, replete with year-round sunshine, blue skies, and the false hope and optimism which defines this part of the world. And while, yes, having been exposed to the harsh reality of the industry and the town I'd become cynical, a glimmer of belief in the dream still lingered, doggedly refusing to be extinguished. It was only when Laura and I drove down the 405 one afternoon to San Pedro with boxes containing my possessions for shipping that the enormity of what I was doing hit home. I was leaving, giving up, with nothing concrete to show for my efforts except memories - some good, others not.

But here again I was guilty of complacency. Of course I had something concrete to show for my time here. I had Laura. I had our relationship. And wasn't it the best possible thing to come out of the experience? Well obviously to me this part of my life didn't count, didn't even belong anywhere on the metaphorical balance sheet I'd drawn up of the past five years. This anyway is how it must have seemed to Laura sitting beside me in the car as

I rambled on.

The boxes were duly shipped out and a couple of weeks later Laura and I flew to Scotland to spend Christmas and New Year at home. We each had Christmas with our respective families, before I travelled to spend New Year with her and her parents. It was my first time meeting them and despite the usual trepidation you might expect in this type of situation, we hit it off. Laura had been worried about the possibility of me and her old man clashing. He was a dyed-in-the-wool conservative, a firm believer in the British Empire and everything it represented in its heyday. But instead of clashing we got on well, able to discuss our obvious political differences over a few drinks without lapsing into argument. This was a first where I was concerned. Maybe maturity wasn't a foreign land after all.

And then it came time for Laura and I to part. It was a moment we'd both been dreading. The night before we'd lain in bed talking for hours about the future, about how happy we'd be in London after she got back from LA and we were reunited.

Now the time had come.

On a dark morning with a bitterly cold wind cutting through us we said our goodbyes at the ferry terminal. She had tears in her eyes, which weren't just due to the wind, as I spent a few minutes reassuring her that everything was going to be all right, that we'd be together again in no time and not to worry. At the top of the gangway I turned and waved before boarding the ferry.

It was the last time I ever saw her.

Four months later she was pregnant and married to another.

Contemporary culture has eliminated both the concept of the public and the figure of the intellectual. Former public spaces – both physical and cultural – are now either derelict or colonized by advertising. A cretinous anti-intellectualism presides, cheerled by expensively educated hacks in the pay of multinational corporations who reassure their bored readers that there is no need to rouse themselves from their interpassive stupor. The informal censorship internalized and propagated by the cultural workers of late capitalism generates a banal conformity that the propaganda chiefs of Stalinism could only ever have dreamt of imposing. Zer0 Books knows that another kind of discourse – intellectual without being academic, popular without being populist – is not only possible: it is already flourishing, in the regions beyond the striplit malls of so-called mass media and the neurotically bureaucratic halls of the academy. Zer0 is committed to the idea of publishing as a making public of the intellectual. It is convinced that in the unthinking, blandly consensual culture in which we live, critical and engaged theoretical reflection is more important than ever before.